A Miracle Named Mark

Based on the Actual Life of Mark J. Hublar

Copyright © 2021 Gregory Hublar.

All rights reserved. No part of this publication may be reproduced, distributed, or transmitted in any form or by any means, including photocopying, recording, or other electronic or mechanical methods, without the prior written permission of the publisher, except in the case of brief quotations embodied in critical reviews and certain other noncommercial uses permitted by copyright law. For permission requests, write to the publisher, addressed "Attention: Permissions Coordinator," at the address below.

ISBN: 978-0-578-85140-2 (Paperback).

Any references to historical events, real people, or real places in the book are my memories from my perspective and from those directly quoted.

Book Cover designed with the help of Vernon Eswine and The Marking Company.

Financial backing provided by a grant from Vocational Rehabilitation Service of Indiana.

Supportive services provided by Portals LLC.

Printed by DiggyPOD, Inc., in the United States of America.

First printing edition 2021.

Publisher: Greg Hublar
greghublar@gmail.com
New Albany, IN 47150

www.markjhublarspeaks.com

This book is dedicated to the countless souls sent to institutions who had no one to speak up for them, as well as the souls which are returned to heaven before taking their first breath, all in the name of Down syndrome.

Table of Contents

Introduction:	Page 1
Chapter 1: Meet the Parents	Page 5
Chapter 2: Here We Go	Page 17
Chapter 3: Not The Same But Not Different	Page 37
Chapter 4: Time To Be A Big Brother	Page 51
Chapter 5: Just One Of The Gang	Page 63
Chapter 6: Where Is Everyone Going	Page 77
Chapter 7: Time To Move On	Page 89
Chapter 8: Unimaginable Blessings	Page 103
Chapter 9: My Time In The Workforce	Page 133
Chapter 10: A Time To Speak Up for Others	Page 155
Chapter 11: The People I Have Met	Page 167
Chapter 12: My Greatest Accomplishments So Far	Page 181
Chapter 13: My Hopes And Aspirations	Page 193
Chapter 13: Acknowledgements	Page 205

Introduction

The decision that Alfred T. Hublar Jr. and Mary Linda Hublar had to unexpectedly make on September 1st 1964 was really no decision at all. On that special day in Indianapolis, they anxiously awaited the birth of their second child Mark Joseph Hublar. Having their first child the year before, expectations could not have been higher. A sibling to their first born, and the second in line with the hope of more to come. This child would now be a welcome addition to a young but growing Catholic family from New Albany, IN.

With the end of another successful pregnancy now at hand, Linda was filled with excitement and more than ready to meet her next child. Would she be having another son? Would she be having her first daughter? Would she look like her mom? Or would he look like his dad? Would he or she have a full head of hair or start off with some beautiful peach fuzz on top. So much love and joy at the thought of bringing another precious life into this world, and more importantly into this family. Excitement filled the air as they anxiously awaited the answers to these and many other questions.

Other than a little less movement on the inside than what she experienced with her first pregnancy, everything appeared to be going as expected. Linda was ready and it was finally time. However, neither Alfred or Linda could have ever imagined how their world was about to be rocked to its core. Nothing and no one could have prepared them for the callous and cold words that would come from the mouths of the medical professionals that had just delivered Mark. And in a flash of disbelief, all their hopes, dreams, and aspirations, that moments before seemed like such a certainty, vanished in an instant.

There was no way for this young couple to have known, or to have had any idea of the journey that had just begun in that very moment. A journey that was not even believed to be possible by any in the medical field at the time, or anywhere else for that matter. A journey that would break down barriers, change minds, warm hearts, and inspire tens of thousands across the country. A journey that was God-Ordained and destined to accomplish His will.

A journey had begun that would so exceed what was believed to even be possible, that this story had to be told. A story of Love. A story of Faith. A story of Hope. A story of Perseverance.

And a story of a Man who would overcome the impossible to not only fulfill his God-given potential, but one who would go on to travel the country advocating for others while helping them find hope to reach their full potential. But to truly attempt to understand this Journey, we must first start at the beginning.

Chapter 1: Meet The Parents

Mary Linda Stemle was born on March 27, 1941 to Joe and Wilma Stemle, a devout Catholic couple from New Albany, Indiana. Joe was the owner of the Stemle Market, a grocery store that was located on Charlestown Road in New Albany. He was a good man who loved his family, worked hard, and enjoyed being a life-long member of the Knights of Columbus. Although a truly honest man by all who knew him, it was a little embellishment regarding his age that ensured Wilma that he was not too young for her.

Some of Linda's fondest memories of her dad were the rides to Salem, Indiana in the Stemle Market grocery truck where they would go to buy fresh eggs for his store. Linda reminisced, "The truck only had a driver's seat so I would sit on a wooden orange crate right next to him. It couldn't have been very comfortable, but how I loved those trips!" That same truck would also be used for loading up Linda's friends and heading to social events. Like the time her dad took her and her friends to ice skate on a then frozen Silver Creek before heading back to the house where Wilma would have homemade donuts and hot chocolate waiting for everyone.

Linda reflected on her dad's generous spirit, remembering a time from her childhood, "He let me bring my friends into his grocery store to pick out popsicles, even after I had mistakenly told them they could have whatever they wanted because everything was free!" Joe's love for Linda remains evident to this day, as a piece of his heart is unknowingly shared with everyone she meets.

Wilma, the disciplinarian of the family, was a school teacher by trade. This empowered her with the skills and confidence needed to provide structure to the family while Joe was at work. It also enabled her to provide homeschooling to Linda when for a time in the second grade she was unable to attend class. "Mother home schooled me then, turning our kitchen into a classroom. I was up and dressed at the regular time, studied every subject, and did every assignment. There were even times set aside for lunch and recess," Linda recalled. "Without my mother's help I would have definitely been held back and would have had to repeat the second grade." Wilma's love for Linda, as well as for all of her children, was always steadfast.

Together, Joe and Wilma demonstrated the meaning of family as they always placed God first, and family above all else. Their love was evident to all whom they encountered. Whether it was providing "Meals on Wheels" to those who could not get out, or in the love they shared in spending time with their many grandchildren, the love of Jesus Christ was always apparent in the way they lived their lives. And though both have long since gone to be with the Lord, Linda lovingly reminisced, "I will always remember the way they made me feel loved and protected."

Mary Linda was named after Mary, the Mother of Jesus. However, she has been called "Linda" her entire life. She was the fifth and final child born to Joe and Wilma. At the time of her birth, Linda joined her 4 older brothers: Jack who was thirteen, Joe who was twelve, Bill who was ten, and Dick who was eight. She was the fulfillment of a dream that appeared would go unfulfilled in Joe and Wilma's life. A long-awaited answer to a simple prayer, that for a daughter to round out the family. But if they were hoping for laces and curls, and all things gentle and calm, boy did they have a surprise waiting for them. To say Linda grew up as anything other than a tomboy would be a great understatement.

Being the youngest sibling, and the only daughter, Linda had to find ways to entertain herself. She spent some of her earliest years learning to cut out paper dolls, coloring, and playing Jacks. She eventually learned how to ride a bike and spent endless hours riding through the neighborhood. She also spent a significant amount of time roller skating in her basement. But these things eventually failed to satisfy the longing Linda felt for both social interactions, as well as more physical activities.

Striving to emulate her brothers, she began climbing trees as well as playing sports with the boys in her neighborhood. She earned a broken leg at the age of eight playing football with her cousins. Two years later she broke her arm going down a slide standing up on her feet. While most would think this is something to be regretted, Linda had a different view. Reflecting back on her being the first to break any bones amongst her siblings, she now had a claim to fame in which the older brothers could not boast.

Linda loved any attention she could garner from her older brothers. Whether it be playing croquet with them in the back yard, or Old Maid around the table. Being included with her brothers was of the utmost importance. Even if this meant she ended up crying, which she recalls frequently happening, because her older brothers would never let her win. Little did she know at the time, these very events were building within her a determination that would prepare her for the challenges that awaited her later in life.

Linda's fondest childhood memories are the times she spent with her brothers, who taught her among other things, how to shoot marbles. She fondly reflected on those days, "My brothers taught me how to shoot them, and even let me use their marbles." Being the youngest sibling by at least eight years, and remembering back on how she would long for the attention of her older brothers, she recalled her favorite memory, "Oh how I loved to swim with them at the old Colonial Club Swimming Pool!" However, what Linda called "swimming with her brothers" really turned out to be her brothers throwing her back and forth to each other like a football. "That was the best time of my life," she exclaimed!

The time Linda got to spend with her brothers was a source of love and strength that was instrumental in giving her the kind of heart that would lead her to one day desire a family of her own. And with the love and support of a solid family, Linda continued to grow. First attending Holy Trinity Grade School in New Albany. And then moving on to Providence High School in Clarksville, Indiana, where she first met Alfred.

After graduating from high school, Linda began studying to be a nurse. She always felt this would be a good way to fulfill her desire to help others. Unfortunately, she quickly learned that the sight of other people's blood was not something she was comfortable with, and so decided not to pursue her degree.

However, at the same time, she was presented with an opportunity to stay at home and help her father through an illness. So, Linda chose to leave school and focus on nursing Joe back to health. And the time she was able to spend with her dad during this time, meant more to her than any degree ever would. Linda never returned to college, as the Lord had bigger plans in store for her.

Alfred "Buddy" Theodore Hublar Jr. was born to Alfred Sr., and Pauline Hublar on March 8th, 1941. He started life as a younger brother to his older sister Joyce. And later he would be joined by his younger brother David, and then by Margaret, the youngest of the four siblings. A family raised in love. Each having their own chores and responsibilities, they were expected to carry their load.

Alfred Sr., Buddy's father, was affectionately known as "Teenie". He was a determined man who was known by those closest to him as a perfectionist. He had a drive and a desire to make and do things to the very best of his ability. A burning desire to do things right, he possessed a drive that is rarely seen today.

Teenie personally built all four homes the family lived in over the years, including installing all the plumbing, heating and electricity. He was a very talented man. And whether succeeding in a life-long career at the Courier Journal, or rerouting 100 yards of a creek with a shovel just to move it a little further from his house, when Tennie set his mind to something, it was going to get done, and it was going to get done right!

Pauline's life got off to a rough start. Losing her mother at a young age, she was required to help support the family any way she could. And well before a young girl should. Instead of playing as most kids did, Pauline would walk five miles to a job where she worked as a seamstress. After manually sewing for hours on end, she would then walk the five miles back to the family home. Hard work and the desire to succeed was the only way for this family. And this work ethic would be instilled into Alfred Jr., and into his siblings.

When asked how he got the nickname "Buddy", Alfred Jr responded, "As long as I can remember I have always been called Buddy. And as I became older, all of my friends and family would call me Buddy, so that just became my name." He recalls not wanting his friends to call him Alfred or Theodore, so Buddy suited him just fine. It wasn't until he arrived at college, where the professors would not refer to students by their nickname, that he became known as Al. These days it is easy to tell his lifelong acquaintances, who refer to him as Buddy, from those who know him more formally, as Al. From this point, we will refer to him interchangeably as Buddy or Al, depending on the situation.

Buddy was truly a chip off the ole block. He had an extremely strong will growing up that some might refer to as extremely stubborn. Childhood stories of Buddy holding his breath when he was unable to get his way are not particularly unique. However, stories of Buddy holding his breath until he literally passed out, are unique. And this became a fairly regular routine when things weren't going his way.

But in true Hublar fashion, Pauline would simply drag his unconscious body over to the water spicket where she would bring him back to the conscious reality that this trick was not going to work. Although Buddy's oxygen deprivation techniques were not particularly effective in the eyes of his mother, it was nevertheless a foreshadowing of the God-Given strength of will that the Lord had given to him in order to meet the challenges that would later unfold in his life.

Buddy started out first grade at Mount Tabor School in New Albany. He remembered soon after, coming home one day and asking his mother questions regarding God. He further recounted how his questions had troubled his mother so badly, that she soon concluded that public school would not be capable of providing the type of spiritual education she wanted for her children. And how she informed Tennie that no matter what it took, she was going to enroll their children in a school where they could freely and fully learn about God. Soon after, Buddy and his siblings were all enrolled at St. Mary Catholic School in New Albany. Three years later they transferred to Our Lady of Perpetual Help, a new parish with a school closer to home.

Growing up, Buddy loved to shoot marbles in the schoolyard at recess. And for a moment he seemingly went back in time, explaining, "The ground was covered in fine cinders that worked well when drawing the circle in which the marbles had to be placed. I had what they referred to at the time as a "Log Roller". It was an extra-large marble that could easily knock the regular sized marbles out of the circle, giving me the best opportunity to win the game." Coming back to the present, Buddy concluded, "I always carried my marbles in an old sock that mother made for me."

In addition to marbles, Buddy enjoyed racing his soap box car. He was very proud of his car and loved to race it as often as he could. His love of racing would lead to a life-long affinity for automobiles. And as he grew up, he could easily tell the make and model of any car just by looking at the taillights. And although he would one day outgrow his ability to race soap box cars, to this day a picture that includes Buddy and his soap box car still hangs in a local tire business in downtown New Albany, testifying to his enduring love for cars.

Buddy went on to attend Our Lady of Providence High School. He enjoyed playing football for the Pioneers and was their starting running back. It is here that he would meet Linda and together would begin their journey of a lifetime. After graduation he headed off to get his undergraduate degree at Purdue University. From there he continued his studies, receiving his MBA from Indiana University.

Together, with Linda, their miraculous journey would soon begin!

Chapter 2: Here We Go

It wasn't long before Buddy and Linda realized they were meant to be together forever. So, after five and half years of dating and a brief engagement, they were married on August 18th, 1962 at Holy Trinity Catholic Church in New Albany.

Now if you are not familiar with the heat and humidity that can occur in this part of the country, just know at times it can be sweltering and downright dangerous. And so it was on this particular day. And with no air conditioning in the church, Linda knew she had to devise a plan to make sure things went off without a hitch. "The bridesmaids and I carried smelling salt capsules in our gloves just in case one of us started to faint," she cleverly recalled. Fortunately, everyone remained upright, and the wedding went on as planned.

It was a beautiful ceremony that was truly a "Hublar Wedding." David Hublar, Buddy's younger and only brother, served as his best man. Buddy's older sister Joyce filled the coveted role of Maid of Honor. And Margaret, his much younger sister, excitedly participated as a Junior Bridesmaid. They were joined by two additional bridesmaids and two additional groomsmen, all of whom were very close friends of both the bride and groom. Even Linda's young niece and nephew served as the flower girl and ring bearer respectively. Family and friends filled the pews as they watched this young couple profess their love for each other. Before God they committed to stay together, come what may, until death would they part.

Unfortunately, Linda's brother Joe just had surgery and was unable to attend the wedding. So, in true family fashion following the ceremony, the wedding party headed across the Ohio River to visit Joe who was recovering in a Louisville hospital. While obviously disappointed at not being able to be there to see his only sister get married, Joe's heart was warmed by their simple act of kindness. With the reception scheduled to begin at 2:00pm, they had just enough time to make Joe feel as if he had actually been to the wedding, and that's exactly what they did!

With their mission accomplished, they now headed back across the bridge to attend their intimate but quaint reception that was being held at Linda's parent's house. With family and friends in attendance, they enjoyed two hours of celebrating filled with laughter and love. A theme that would not only resonate throughout their married life, but also one that would be a major source of strength that would see them through any storm. Soon it was time to wave goodbye to their family and friends and turn their sights onto the highly anticipated honeymoon; a trip to Daytona Beach, Florida!

Sometimes life has a funny way of playing out just a little different than what we anticipated, or what we had envisioned. Sometimes it's the little details we overlook or fail to consider that brings us back to reality. As was the case when it was time to change into their traveling clothes to begin the long journey down to sunny Florida. "I guess it was too new for me to share the same room in order to change our clothes, so we did so in separate rooms," Linda modestly recalled. Times were different then, when couples actually waited to enjoy some of the more intimate benefits of being married, until they were actually married.

In any case, the first awkward situation that can occur with any new married couple, was now in the rearview mirror! Unfortunately, the second was just around the corner. As the confident couple crossed the Ohio River into Kentucky and headed down I-65 South, it wasn't long before both of them realized they had no idea how to get to Florida, let alone Daytona Beach. This prompted a humble but necessary call from the newly minted husband to his father-in-law for a little assistance. Back in the car with the directions they needed, these honeymooners once again headed south towards their ultimate destination!

After several hours in the car, it was time to stop for dinner, and to start thinking of a place to spend their first night together as husband and wife. With no meal too good for this special occasion, but also a desire to keep moving down the road, it was a couple of chili dogs and root beers to go from Dairy Queen that served as the first meal for this newly married couple. Soon they had made it to Nashville, TN which certainly seemed like a great place to choose a hotel for their special night. Little did they know that Saturday Night in the Music City was the busiest night of the week due in large part to the Grand Ole Opry.

Pulling into the first Holiday Inn he could find, Buddy anxiously went to the counter to choose a room for their wedding night. Unfortunately, there were no rooms available as it was completely sold out. The clerk understanding the seriousness of the situation, began calling all the other Holiday Inns in the area but was met with the same lack of vacancies. He then went above and beyond by calling his competitors until he finally found a room at the Capitol Park Inn. Buddy was finally off the hook as a disastrous situation was narrowly avoided.

After attending Sunday Mass, and following a quick breakfast, it was back into the car. They continued racking up the miles, making it deep into the state of Georgia. And this time they found a motel without any hassle! The next morning, it was back into the car for a third consecutive day of traveling. At this point they were more than ready to start feeling the hot sun on their faces and the warm sand between their toes!

It was all business from that point forward, as neither one of them could wait to get there! So, Buddy and Linda took turns driving the rest of the way to Florida. "One time I remember changing drivers while still driving down the highway without even stopping," Linda sheepishly recalled. "We must have been in a hurry!"

On the evening of the third consecutive day of traveling, Buddy and Linda finally made it to Daytona Beach, Florida! "We couldn't believe we had made it all the way to Florida," Linda proudly exclaimed. It was almost dark when the weary travelers arrived, so they stopped at the first motel they saw with a vacancy sign. However, it happened to be across the road from the ocean. Which meant it wasn't exactly close enough to the ocean for this excited couple.

So, the next day they decided to find a place to spend the remainder of their honeymoon that was actually located on the beach. The Copacabana was a two-story yellow building that was right on the ocean, and it contained a full kitchen. This was perfect as it allowed them to save money by cooking their own meals. They enjoyed that location so much that it became the destination spot for many future family vacations. With a gleam in her eye, Linda reminisced, "It was a wonderful honeymoon that was worth every mile we had spent in the car. We loved the ocean and spent most of our first day just laying out on the beach!"

However, the next lesson these newlyweds were about to learn was awaiting them the very next morning, as they awoke to a stinging reminder of just how much fun they had out in the sun. "We paid the price by getting the worst sunburn of our lives,"

Linda painfully remembers. "The only thing we wanted to touch our skin for the next couple of days was Noxzema, which we used as a sunburn reliever".

But to know Buddy and Linda, is to know that a little discomfort could never stop them from having a good time! They made several trips to the Boardwalk, which was just a couple of short miles down the beach from where they were staying. It had rides and an arcade with lots of games to play. There was also a long pier they enjoyed walking out on as it led them far out into the ocean and above the breaking waves below. One night they found themselves at a live auction on the Boardwalk where they won a prize for being married the shortest amount of time – less than a week.

Linda remembers the feeling of empowerment she felt as she quickly began to realize they were all alone and could do whatever they wanted, whenever they wanted. She recalled the liberating feelings at the thought of finally being on her own and how she was truly becoming independent. And never more so than one night around midnight, when they were both hungry, leaving their ocean front motel and going out for a hamburger. Linda explained, "Having the freedom to do that made me realize that we were truly married, and that we were in charge of making our own decisions. No more curfews and family rules." Laughingly she concluded, "I was really beginning to like married life!"

And that was a very good thing. Particularly since, as happens on all vacations, the fun and temporary break from the everyday responsibilities, would soon be coming to an end. At least for now. It was time to begin the long journey back to Indiana where they would continue their new life as husband and wife. The time had gone by so fast, but the memories would literally last a lifetime. Seven years would go by before they were able to return to this treasured location. And return they did on many occasions. But, oh how life would change for these newlyweds!

Back home in New Albany, far from the relaxing sound of breaking waves and the feel of warm sand between their toes, it was time for Buddy to return to Purdue University in West Layfette, Indiana where he was currently a full-time student.

Buddy had started his college career studying Engineering. This was largely due to the urging of his father. However, Buddy quickly discovered that he hated engineering, but did like to work with his hands. So, he switched to Aviation Technology and earned an associate degree.

He went on to graduate, receiving a bachelor of science degree with honors from the School of Industrial Education, majoring in Industrial Supervision. However, this would now require the newlyweds to live in the married student apartments for two years, instead of the one year they had previously planned.

Buddy and Linda took residence in the married student apartments on Nimitz Drive. They lived in a two-room apartment, with a full bath. The kitchen and living room combined to account for one of the two rooms, while the bedroom accounted for the other. There was a large bamboo curtain that could be pulled across the width of the kitchen to conceal the appliances. The living room contained a couch, an overstuffed chair, a coffee table, a TV table on wheels, and a very small TV. Most of the furniture pieces were hand-me-downs from their parents, including a bedroom suite consisting of a bed, a dresser, and a small desk that filled the bedroom. Linda summarized, "In my eyes, we had everything we needed!

Thankfully for these struggling newlyweds, Buddy's father was able to cover both the cost of the tuition, as well as the eighty-one dollars each month for rent, that also included all the utilities. That October Linda started a new job at National Homes just off campus and was proud to contribute wherever she could. "Most of my paycheck went for our phone bills, groceries, gasoline, books, and the occasional pizza or night out." She continued, "Some of the best times we had were free. After Sunday Mass we would have a picnic in our favorite spot next to the White River. And the rest of the week was spent working and studying."

Visits from family and friends living in New Albany were always a welcomed occasion. Every time Linda's parents would come to Purdue, they would bring a care package from the Stemle Market. "It was a huge box filled with things like meat, cheese, and even pickles, especially since they knew how much Buddy loved pickles!"

It was also not unusual for Linda to find an envelope under her pillow containing a twenty-dollar bill, shortly after her parents would leave to return to New Albany. Thinking back on those times, Linda said, "I think our families were afraid for us. But being young and naïve, we had no fear whatsoever!"

For entertainment, Buddy and Linda would go to football games whenever the Boilermakers were playing at home. They also enjoyed attending concerts, going on picnics, sleigh rides, and even ice skating whenever the tennis courts would become iced over.

Their best friends on campus were Louis and Janet Marlow, another couple from New Albany. The four of them spent time together playing cards, attending social events and just being there for each other, as close friends do. Linda and Janet even worked together at National Homes. Having close friends on campus was especially important. Particularly since back then traveling home took roughly five hours. So, understandably those trips were few and far between.

Case in point, although Linda and Janet both had Thanksgiving Day off from work, anyone who didn't show up the day after, would not receive their holiday pay. That meant these two young ladies would have to figure out a new way to celebrate the holiday, separated from family and friends back home. So, they decided to make the best of it. And along with Buddy and Louis, celebrated their first Thanksgiving together.

These were special times as the young couple continued to adapt to married life and being away from their families. Nowadays Linda looks back on those special times with a deep sense of gratitude for their early friendships. "Occasionally, Buddy and I will still dust off the home movies we took that day. And it always makes us laugh!"

Starting a family had always been in the plans for Buddy and Linda. While both of them felt having somewhere around four to six children would make the perfect size family, they were willing to accept whatever the good Lord had in store for them. Thinking back Buddy recalled, "I thought four or five children would be a nice size family, and like most newlyweds at the time, I thought an equal number of boys and girls would be nice." He continued, "But we would accept any number of children that God would bless us with!" So ready to take the next step on their journey, they set their sights on starting a family.

Linda remembers wanting to start a family right away and she had no reason to believe that wouldn't be the case. However, In December, four months after they were married, she was beginning to worry. "My mother had always told me that it only takes "one time" to get pregnant, but that didn't seem to be the case with us." She nervously continued: "I had been in a head-on car wreck three months before the wedding, and now thought maybe that was the reason I wasn't getting pregnant?"

She had good reason to be concerned as the very same thing had happened to her sister-in-law. Linda somberly explained, "After being in a car accident, Margie was not able to have children. So, she and my brother ended up adopting three wonderful babies." Linda concluded by saying, "I thought maybe Buddy and I would be doing the same thing one day."

Times were a lot different back then as there were no convenient take home tests that could privately and instantly answer one of the most confidential questions a young couple will ever ask. Only those couples, and I dare say particularly the mom in waiting, could ever understand the empty feelings that can range from despair, to sadness, to frustration, and even to feelings of false guilt and shame that can follow a disappointing trip to the doctor's office. But Linda's doctor continued to be a source of encouragement, telling her, "Everything is fine. Just relax and let nature take its course."

Relying on their faith, and the assurance of the doctor that there was nothing physically stopping them from becoming pregnant, Buddy and Linda remained faithful. They knew full well that the Lord was in control and that His will would be done. It was just the challenge of trying to understand His will, and preparing mentally for whatever His will might mean for their hopes of starting a family, that made some days a little harder than others.

But sure enough, in the following month, it finally happened! And two months later the doctor confirmed that they would be having their first child in October!

Linda joyfully recalled celebrating the good news, explaining, "Buddy took me out to a very nice restaurant. And I remember large bowls of shrimp on the salad bar, which we filled our plates with a couple of times. It was a wonderful night and we had a wonderful meal!"

However, as was mentioned earlier in this book, sometimes it's the little details that are overlooked that can keep life interesting. As it was when it came time to pay the bill and Buddy anxiously discovered he was a little short on cash! But through the grace of God, who was not going to allow anything to take away the joy of this wonderful night, one of the waiters happened to be a classmate and friend of Buddy's. He willingly loaned Buddy the couple of dollars needed to cover the shortfall. And a potentially embarrassing situation was averted!

In March of 1963, both Buddy and Linda celebrated their 22nd birthdays. Buddy continued going to classes every day, and Linda continued to work at National Homes. After summer classes were over, they went home for a short visit. And while in New Albany, Linda's mother brought out a small crib on wheels that she had used thirty-five years before when Linda's brothers were just babies. "She gave it to us to keep," Linda exclaimed! "Buddy repaired one of the wooden wheels that had broken, and together we scraped off the old paint before painting it white. We even added little lamb decals to it!"

And after buying lots of diapers, a rocking chair, and other essentials that any first-time expectant parents would most likely need, they were almost ready for their new arrival, and the start of their much-anticipated family!

Back on campus, Buddy's friend Louie Marlow had now graduated, and he and his wife Janet moved back to New Albany. However, two other couples who were attending Purdue University, that happened to also hail from New Albany, would now provide a sense of family while filling the important need for friendship. Larry and Margaret Burke, and Chizzie and Karen Wolf became Buddy and Linda's new partners in crime and would remain life-long friends. "We had some great times together," both Linda and Buddy exclaimed!

Like the first home football game which was known as "Senior Cord Day." The seniors wore bright yellow, hand painted, corduroy pants, a derby bowl hat, and carried a curved handle bamboo walking cane. Linda sheepishly recalled, "Larry even helped Buddy paint his cords, although some of it may have been a little X-rated. She continued, "It was such a fun day! All the seniors got to parade on the field showing off their original and unusual senior cords!" According to Linda, the only drawback to that day was the heat, "I was well into my pregnancy and remember seeing another expectant mother having to be carried out after she fainted, and I was praying that wouldn't happen to me!" Linda's fear soon dissipated as she safely made it off the field and quickly began cooling down.

With excitement and anticipation growing, the days continued to pass as the calendar drew closer to the October 4th due date. Until finally the big day had arrived and they would soon be meeting their first-born child. However, as the hours continued to pass on that long-awaited day, so did the excitement. It soon became apparent the celebration would have to wait at least another day. And then another. And then another. And Another.

Knowing the frustration and disappointment their friends were feeling, Chizzie and Karen took the expectant couple out for ice cream and a long ride in the back seat of their car. Linda laughing recalled, "Chizzie must have driven over every set of railroad tracks he could think of to help get things started." Well, it must have worked, because later that night Linda's time had finally arrived!

Buddy and Linda welcomed their first child, Michael Alfred Hublar into the world on October 8, 1963. Mike, as he has always been called, was a happy, healthy baby boy who would soon be introduced to the rest of his family. That weekend both sets of grandparents traveled to Purdue to meet their newest grandson. Buddy recalls the knock on the door and how proud they were to show off the new addition to the family. "We opened the door and held Mike up under his arms. But since we really didn't know how to put diapers on correctly, his diaper immediately fell off as we raised him up to show him off". This prompted a chuckle by the arriving guests to which one of them quickly remarked "Well we can see he is a boy."

In all fairness to these first-time parents, diapers at the time were made of cloth and required the use of safety pins. This obviously required a little more skill then simply pressing down on the Velcro tabs used today on the more common disposable diapers.

Birth announcements were soon on the way to all of their friends back home in New Albany, as they couldn't wait to proudly share news of the birth of their newborn son! Buddy fondly recalled his hopes for this child, "I prayed that he would have a successful and happy life!" Being the first Hublar to go to college himself, one of Buddy's major goals for this child, as well as for all of his future children, is that they too would all go to college.

Buddy's father always valued an education and instilled into him the importance of making sure he earned a degree. That is why Teenie worked so hard to pay for Buddy's education. Buddy proudly recalled the directive, and the reasoning behind his father's belief, saying, "Dad frequently told me to get as much education as I possibly could because it is something no one can ever take away from you." Experiencing the Great Depression, Buddy's dad had learned self-reliance and the value of hard work. And he felt it was imperative that a formal education be a part of the Hublar legacy.

Speaking of hard work, it was time for Buddy to get back to his school work, while also learning how to be a good father. He would soon have to learn how to balance the demands of getting his degree with the desire of wanting to spend time with his family. And Linda quickly began learning her new role as a stay-at-home mother, while also continuing to be a loving and supportive wife. Ready or not, life was moving forward and Buddy and Linda's journey of a lifetime just took a major step forward!

Chapter 3: Not The Same But Not Different

Life continued for Buddy and Linda, and they excitedly embraced their new role as father and mother. They were confident the Lord would always lead and provide for them. And that they would successfully grow into their new role of being a parent. Their love for each other, and their faith in Jesus Christ, became the bedrock of their family. Underneath it all was their unwavering belief that as long as they were together, they would figure it out, come what may. And that was a great thing. Particularly since what was coming next was another baby!

But how could this be, they thought? It literally took several months of trying to get pregnant the first time before they achieved their goal. The doubt and worry they experienced then, and the fear that it was never going to happen, now seemed like a distant and faint memory. But now within less than two months of bringing home their first born, Linda was pregnant again. Maybe Linda's mother was right after all when she prophetically said "It only takes one time to get pregnant." Ready or not, Buddy and Linda's life was about to get a whole lot more interesting as this young family would soon be increasing by one.

The initial shock of knowing their family would be growing a lot quicker than they had originally imagined was soon replaced with the overwhelming love that filled their hearts at the thought of bringing another precious life into this world. The idea of another "Hublar" in the family, and a companion for Mike, was something that Buddy and Linda quickly warmed up to. Even though this meant they would soon be in the unique position of having two babies under the age of one, the couple remained fearless and faithful that the Lord would provide for them. And soon it was time to put the focus back where it belonged, attending to the needs of Mike, the newest addition to the family.

Mike continued to grow and bring all the joy that a new baby brings, particularly a first-born baby. All the wonder and excitement that accompany every "first" that a new baby will experience. The first smile. The first giggle. The first eye contact. The first feeding. The first belch. The first throw up. And yes, even the first diaper change.

All of these seemingly simple acts somehow have a miraculous and wondrous quality in the eye of a first-time parent. It's these experiences that help form the special bond between a child and a parent. It is also some of these same experiences that somehow lovingly empower the parent to wake from a deep sleep to attend to their child's needs, when the average superhero would fail miserably.

Time continued to move quickly, as the excitement of watching Mike grow filled their days. And thoughts of what was to come with the blessing of another child, filled their nights. Mike, born perfectly healthy as expected, continued to pass one milestone after another. Whether it was rolling over, sitting up, or learning to crawl, Mike progressed just like a little baby is supposed to. And with each passing day, this young couple's confidence and belief in their parenting skills continued to grow. Life was good and their love for each other, and for their growing family, continued to deepen.

Preparations were already underway as a new crib was set up next to Mike's crib. Bottles, formula, diapers, and little newborn outfits were ready and waiting for the newest addition to the family. Linda fondly recalled, "It was a very happy time for me, because I knew Mike would have a little brother or sister to play with, and he wouldn't have to grow up alone."

Buddy and Linda's imaginations were understandably starting to run wild as they began to imagine all the good times ahead. Linda shared one such thought, "The baby was due on Sept. 14th, the same date as my oldest brother Jack's birthday. And I remember imaging what it might be like having joint parties at my parent's house!"

Both Linda and Buddy were filled with excitement and more than ready to meet their next child. Would they be having another son? Would they be having their first daughter? Would she look like Linda? Or would he look like Buddy? Would he or she have a full head of hair or start off with some beautiful peach fuzz on top? There was so much love and joy at the thought of bringing another precious life into this world, and more importantly into this family. Excitement filled the air as they anxiously awaited the answers to these and many other questions. However, they apparently weren't the only ones excited to meet, as this baby decided it couldn't wait any longer and started the process two weeks early!

The time had now arrived and this baby was ready to come into the world. By having gone through labor just eleven months earlier with Mike, Linda wasn't nervous. "I knew from experience that there would be pain, but after a few hours, there would be tremendous joy," she exclaimed! Linda remained confident even though her regular doctor was out of town for the Labor Day weekend, and a new doctor would be handling the delivery.

With Buddy by her side, she endured the six hours of labor, which on a positive note was considerably shorter than the labor she endured with Mike. In any case, it was time for the delivery which meant Buddy would have to leave her side and be relegated to the waiting room.

"I was completely knocked out during the delivery," Linda said. When she awoke after the delivery, she found herself in a semi-private room shared by another mother and her newborn. Linda could hardly wait to meet her new bundle of joy and share this most sacred of moments with Buddy. However, time continued to pass, and this long-awaited meeting seemed to be somehow delayed. "It seemed like hours and I still hadn't got to hold my baby," Linda sadly recounted. "I asked a nurse when my baby would be brought to me and she informed me the doctor wanted to talk to me first. "That was my first moment of fear!"

Finally, the doctor came into the room where this now understandably nervous young couple was waiting. Separated from their precious baby they had still yet to hold, this mostly unfamiliar person spoke words they could have never imagined. "Your son has Mongolism," the doctor said. These words were followed by his crushing prediction, "He will never walk, he will never talk, He will never show any emotion, and he will ruin your family!"

Following that professional medical prognosis came a sincere but misguided attempt of comfort in assuring them that this baby would be well cared for by simply leaving him behind in the care of professionals. And in a flash of disbelief, all of their hopes, dreams and aspirations, that hours before seemed like such a certainty, vanished in an instant.

So, what in the world is Mongolism you might ask? The Merriam-Webster Dictionary defines it as being: "Characteristic of a race of humankind native to Asia and classified according to physical features." These features seem to be spelled out a little more clearly in this same company's definition of Down syndrome in which they define as: "A congenital condition characterized especially by developmental delays, usually mild to moderate impairment in cognitive functioning, short stature, upward slanting eyes, a flattened nasal bridge, broad hands with short fingers, decreased muscle tone, and by trisomy of the human chromosome numbered 21."

The Mayo Clinic has defined Down syndrome as: "A genetic disorder caused when abnormal cell division results in an extra full or partial copy of chromosome 21." And they assert it is this extra genetic material that causes the developmental changes and physical features of those with Down syndrome. They go on to note that Down syndrome varies in severity among individuals, and causes them to have a lifelong intellectual disability and developmental delays. And unfortunately, they conclude that it also commonly causes other medical abnormalities, including heart and gastrointestinal disorders. It's currently the most common genetic chromosomal disorder and cause of learning disabilities in children.

According to the National Association for Down syndrome, "During the first half of the twentieth century in the United States, the majority of children with Down syndrome were placed in institutions – frequently right after birth. This resulted in great human suffering for those individuals and for their families, who were convinced, often by members of the medical community, that the child was less than human and that their needs would be so great, their families would not be able to raise them." They went on to explain, "These children were "warehoused" in large state institutions – often in deplorable conditions – locked away so that the rest of society could not see the horror of their lives."

This was the climate that Buddy and Linda were faced with when they brought, Mark Joseph Hublar, into the world! But to know Buddy and Linda, is to know there was no way they were leaving that hospital without their beautiful baby boy. Buddy defiantly recounted, "Linda and I agreed that we would take Mark home and love him as we did our other kids – regardless of how many we had!" He continued, "We felt like that if this is what God wants, then He would help us get through this. And we agreed that we would continue to work together to help Mark have as good a life as possible based on his capabilities."

Armed only with their faith in God and their unwavering love for each other, they took Mark home. Ready or not, their journey into the great unknown of raising a child with Down syndrome had just begun! They knew from the very beginning that Mark would be loved just as Mike was loved. With virtually no information available on the subject, the plan was to raise him similar to the way they had been raising Mike. And to trust God that everything would work out according to His will!

Al took a moment and deeply reflected back on the prayer he prayed at the first Sunday mass in New Albany, following the birth of Mark. "Lord, please give Mark enough intelligence to be able to know, love, and serve you. And, I promise that I will do everything possible to help him have a full life, and to help him do whatever he is capable of doing." Little did Al know at the time how that prayer would be answered in such an incredible way!

Days turned into weeks and weeks turned into months, as life continued moving forward for this growing family. Mark, while physically healthy, was understandably delayed in many areas of development common to other babies. Al explained, "Mark started out with very little body strength and therefore could not sit up, crawl, or do the other things that babies his age could do." "However," Linda remarked, "His eyes were always open as if he was observing everyone and everything." Mark was a quick learner right from the start and it wasn't long before strange things started happening that began to cast doubt upon the grim future the doctor had previously predicted.

Al cited the following example, "I can remember one day when we were physically supporting him as he was trying to stay upright in a sitting position. We decided to experiment a bit by removing our hands from him and to see what would happen? And much to our amazement, Mark had somehow learned how to remain in an upright position on his own!"

They quickly remembered that this simple act was one of many things the doctors said that Mark would never be able to do on his own. Optimism began to grow as they thought to themselves, "If the doctors were wrong about this, then how many other things would Mark be able to do that the doctors didn't think he would?"

Linda remembers how Mark loved to be held and to be rocked. And how he loved listening to Disney audio stories. But she also noticed that he seemed to be following along as though he was somehow keeping up with the story. So, she tried a little experiment, explaining, "When you heard the chiming sound that Tinkerbell would make, it meant it was time to turn the page.

Sometimes, I would deliberately hesitate just to see Mark look up at me as if to say, 'It's time to turn the page'."

And with each passing day it seemed like Mark was reaching another milestone, surpassing an expectation, and generally displaying that he had more potential than he was originally credited with. One specific thing it seemed that the doctors failed to consider was the positive impact an older brother would have on Mark. A brother he loved to play with, show affection to, learn from, and generally try to do anything that he would do.

Mike filled the role of a loving and caring brother who would continually mentor Mark just by doing the normal everyday things a boy tends to do. Linda recalled how Mike was the leader and Mark was the follower, saying, "Mike would pick out the toys they were going to play with and Mark learned how to play with them by watching Mike." Mike was also instrumental in teaching Mark many other things, including how to crawl. Miraculously Mark even learned how to walk at the age of two. This was a very big milestone, and yet another medical prediction that Mark proved to be false.

Next up for Mark was the challenge of learning how to talk. Mark had learned to point at the things that he wanted, and would even gesture for emphasis. However, encouraged and empowered by Mark's previous achievements, Buddy and Linda felt it was time to challenge Mark even further. And at the age of four, they took him to a speech therapist. The therapist, recognizing that Mark was understanding the language, but was not trying to use words, came up with a simple suggestion that proved invaluable.

Linda explained, "He told us to pretend that we did not understand what Mark was asking for, unless he at least tried to say the word. It was hard to understand him most of the time, but it got better as time went on." She continued, "At times I felt as though he was teaching us his language more than he was learning ours, but it wasn't long until he was able to put sentences together. And once he learned how to talk, that's all he wanted to do!" She laughingly concluded, "Maybe he was making up for lost time."

Almost everything the first doctor said about Mark's initial capabilities turned out to be wrong. And with each new milestone passed, it gave this young couple a much brighter outlook for Mark's future. Milestones that included sitting up, crawling, eating from a spoon, being potty trained, walking, and even talking, would turn out to be mere precursors to future accomplishments that were unimaginable at the time.

These future accomplishments would include such things as reading, writing, playing sports, going to school and so much more. All of which they were previously told would never happen. Linda gratefully reflected, "Each new accomplishment seemed like a miracle to us. And with God's help and his brother's influence, we knew Mark was on his way to living a very fulfilling and normal life."

At this point in time, there was no question Mark was quickly becoming more alike than he was different.

Chapter 4: Time To Be A Big Brother

Mark continued to grow and progress beyond anything the doctors had predicted. He was now walking and talking, and showing all kinds of emotions. He loved to laugh, smile, hug, learn, rough house with Mike, and do almost anything a young boy would do. Mark even began attending The Noble School in Indianapolis when he was just two years old. There he would learn colors, numbers, shapes, games, and how to play with other children. While attending this school, Mark also picked up an affection for singing. Though he would mostly hum the words, he became especially fond of Christmas songs.

The Noble School was founded in 1953 by parents of children with developmental disabilities. Similar to Buddy and Linda, Noble's founders ignored the doctor's advice, as well as societal pressures. They were convinced that their special needs children could not only learn, but could one day realize their dreams and contribute significantly to the world around them. Not only were they right, but the organization these parents founded has dramatically expanded and is still servicing the Central Indiana Community to this day. More information on this organization can be found at www.mynoblelife.com

Linda remembers Mark's teacher telling her how she was amazed at just how well Mark played with the other children, and how well he interacted with them. Particularly since that was very unusual for a two-year-old. Buddy and Linda's hearts were warmed by how easily Mark would show affection to those around him. They were also quick to give credit elsewhere for Mark's achievements. A trait that continues to this day.

Case in point, as Linda reflected back on that moment, she said, "I'm sure Mark learned how to play fair with others from Mike, because he did not treat Mark special at home. Mike expected Mark to play by the rules, just the same as he himself had to do." She continued, "Mark had already learned so much from Mike, and he was always eager to try anything that Mike could do. We were thrilled to see Mark's confidence begin to soar, particularly as he learned to better communicate!" And as Mark continued to succeed, they felt compelled to expose him to new challenges.

Buddy and Linda stayed true to their commitment to take Mark as far as he was capable of going. They always allowed him to try new things and did not treat him any different than Mike. And the more challenges they allowed Mark to experience, the more he continued to amaze them. And since they treated Mark no different than Mike, they therefore expected no less of him. They knew in most cases it would take Mark a little longer to accomplish the same goals they would ultimately set for all their children. But they were committed to making sure he was allowed to fail, while always encouraging him to keep trying until he achieved the task at hand. They didn't lower their standards or compromise their expectations of Mark. They were committed to helping him succeed. Even though at times that meant they would have to endure the heartbreak of watching Mark struggle just to achieve the daily activities that most parents are blessed to unknowingly take for granted.

It can conjure up images of the butterfly who struggles mightily to breakout of the cocoon. And how any well-intentioned person with a big heart would be inclined to help by tearing just a little hole in the cocoon to allow it to escape. Never realizing the struggle of the butterfly to free itself is exactly what the Lord had intended to happen. Why God would seemingly allow someone to struggle is a question that only faith and time can answer.

But in the case of the butterfly, the struggle has a definite and life-giving purpose. All the fluttering that occurs in the cocoon actually strengthens the butterfly's wings. And in God's perfect timing, at the exact moment the butterfly is strong enough to fly, it is also strong enough to break out of its cocoon. And if those standards were lessened by being assisted out of its cocoon by a well-intentioned person, that butterfly would surely die, as it would not yet be strong enough to fly on its own.

Speaking of flying, Mark has always soared above all expectations. And this includes being an excellent big brother. But to really understand how Mark came to be the kind of big brother that those closest to him know him to be, we must first take a look at how, and from whom, he learned to become a big brother. And that has a whole lot to do with the time Mark spent with his older brother Mike, especially during his formative years.

Mark always loved playing with Mike and learning from him. Mark tried to imitate everything Mike did. If Mike tried something new, Mark always had the desire, and the courage, to try it too. Linda fondly remembers the times when Mike would teach Mark how to crawl. "Mike knew how to walk, but he would get on his hands and knees to show Mark how it was done. He would keep putting Mark's knees on the floor and then get in front of him to demonstrate how to do it. Weeks and weeks went by, until one day, Mark actually learned how to crawl!"

Linda also enjoys reminiscing about the time when Mike began riding a bicycle, and would stop to teach Mark how to ride the tricycle that had previously been his. She explained, "Mike would keep putting Mark's feet on the pedals and then would push him from behind saying, 'You can do it!'" Mike would do this over and over again until one day Mark really could do it. And soon Mark actually began riding the tricycle by himself!"

Buddy also remembers many great things that Mike taught Mark. Many of which would in effect lay the groundwork for the role Mark would soon play as an older brother himself. But he also remembers some of the things Mike taught Mark that, shall we say, didn't make the "Good List". Such as the time Mike taught Mark how to climb out of his crib at night. Buddy explained, "One night we realized someone was up playing in their room after we had put them down for the night. And as I approached their bedroom, Mike had scurried back into his bed, leaving Mark to answer for himself as to why he was not in his crib". Buddy laughingly said, "Mike taught him how to get out of his crib, but failed to teach him how to get back into his crib." It wouldn't be long before these two partners in crime would take their climbing skills to a whole new level.

Like the time this dynamic duo made a brazen escape from the safety of their back yard out into the great unknown. Linda reluctantly opened up about the escape saying: "Mike was a major climber and he taught Mark how to climb out of our fenced in back yard by climbing over the gate." She continued, "The two climbed over the fence and walked five houses down the block and right into a small creek. Mike came running home and said, "You know that boy what's named Mark? He fell in the creek!"

Linda went on to recall how she and Buddy frantically ran to the creek praying the whole way, "I could hear Mark crying, so I knew he was alive!" When the panicked couple quickly arrived at the creek, they found Mark wet, and with a scratch on his knee. But other than that, he was fine. Linda concluded by saying; "Thankfully, as it turned out at that particular time, the water was only about three inches deep!" But from that day forward she knew she would have to stay one step ahead of these two boys who were quickly becoming best of friends.

Looking back, Mike recounted how he enjoyed always playing with Mark and teaching him everything that he himself was learning. He shared, "In our early childhood years, I loved having a full-time playmate and teaching him everything that I was learning about the world." Mike went on to say, "Our parents made sure that Mark would not be treated any differently because he had Down syndrome, and we certainly didn't give him any special treatment because of it. In many ways this made it much easier for me to just be his big brother without any concern for if I was doing it right." Mike concluded by saying, "The experience of having younger brothers, including one with Down syndrome, has been one of the many blessings in my life."

Time continued to pass, as it always seems to do. And life was good again. The "new normal" this couple had to adjust to only a few short years earlier, had become just the "normal" for this growing family of four. Mike continued teaching Mark anything that he himself would learn. And in turn, Mark continued to love learning everything that Mike would teach him.

Before anyone knew it, three years had already come and gone since receiving that devastating and seemingly inaccurate prognosis they received back in September of 1964. But soon

Buddy and Linda would learn that their family of four would be increasing by one. And the two boys would now have to make room for another sibling.

Buddy and Linda had always stayed true to their promise to the Lord in accepting however many children He was willing to bless them with. So, when they learned that another Hublar baby was on the way, all the same excitement and curiosity of what the Lord might have in store for them began to fill their hearts all over again. Would this be their first daughter? Could this possibly be a third consecutive son? Would he or she be healthy and considered "Normal?" Or would they be faced with another potential soul shaking experience that would lead them down yet another great unknown path?

To say there wasn't real concern as to what this next child would be like, and the challenges that could potentially be awaiting them, would be less than genuine, and certainly not honest. Who in their right mind wouldn't be just a little scared after receiving such a cold and callous prognosis from the so-called experts during their last birthing experience? Who, after being told their newborn son, just hours old, would never walk, talk, sit up, eat from a spoon, never show any emotion and would effectively "ruin your family", wouldn't be a little sick to their stomach when preparing for what they might possibly be told this time around?

However, this is precisely when faith steps in and gently reminds us that no matter the severity of the storm that might be going on around you, Jesus will never forsake you or abandon you. And that is the road that Buddy and Linda chose to continue walking down as they remained upbeat and optimistic throughout this pregnancy. And on May 30th, 1968, Buddy and Linda would give birth to a third son. A healthy baby boy whom they named Gregory Scott Hublar.

However, this time around the first words that Linda heard coming out of the doctor's mouth were, "You have got a tiger!" The relief and joy of hearing those words in that very moment is something that cannot adequately be explained. And while they were more than prepared to accept whatever the Lord had planned for them; the indescribable relief of that long-awaited exhale is something that still can bring a smile to their face today!

As they brought home this newest addition to the family, Buddy and Linda were filled with joy and excitement. Embarking on the task of raising three son's no doubt meant that the wild times they had already experienced with the first two boys, was about to get a little wilder.

Mike and Mark both received their younger brother into their lives, and into their hearts, just as one would hope. Each taking turns holding the newborn, one could only imagine the thoughts that were going through their minds. One thought that is safe to assume, is the thought of how Mark now was able to match Mike in yet another aspect of life; that of being an older brother!

Mark loved Greg from the moment he saw him. He loved being a big brother and wanted to hold him and give him his bottle whenever he could. Linda vividly recalled how when she would tell Mark that the baby needed to be changed, he would run into the other room and bring her a new diaper. "He loved to help with anything that had to do with Greg," Linda said. She also recalled how it would upset Mark every time he would hear Greg crying, "If I wasn't fast enough to tend to Greg any time he cried, Mark would come running to let me know that he was crying."

Buddy also recalled how Mark loved to teach Greg everything he had learned, and was continuing to learn from Mike. This included how to hold his own bottle, how to crawl, how to walk, how to write, and even how to talk. Mark and Greg would spend hours playing together each day and Greg was learning directly from Mark.

However, similar to some of Mike's teachings, not everything that Mark passed on to Greg, shall we say, was super beneficial. Such as teaching Greg how to climb out of his crib, for example. Laughingly, Buddy said, "Greg even learned how to talk from Mark, in Mark's own language. And as a result, we had to send them both to speech therapy."

The two quickly became inseparable. And with Mike now in Pre-School and making his own new friends, Greg came along at just the right time and filled the gap perfectly for Mark.

Buddy and Linda came to realize that the doctors couldn't have possibly foreseen the positive impact that actually being an older brother would ultimately have on Mark and his development. The sense of empowerment and accomplishment one feels when being in a position of actually helping someone else, certainly seemed to be overlooked in Mark's prognosis.

Buddy reflected back on this special time in his life and said, "I believe in Mark's case, being an older brother helped him to advance himself." Buddy went on to say, "It is said that if you want to learn a new skill, you must try and teach it to someone else. And as an older brother, Mark definitely tried to teach Greg new skills!"

Chapter 5: Just One Of The Gang

Mark continued to cherish his role as an older brother to Greg, while continuing to learn everything he could from Mike. He loved the dynamic of now having two brothers in his life. One that would challenge him to learn and to do more. And one in which he could pass on everything that he was learning.

Even now it's difficult not to wonder, if the doctors could have somehow magically peered into the future to see how Mark would so lovingly interact with his brothers, if they might have painted a slightly less desolate picture of his future? In any case, Mark was thriving and growing in every way a young boy could. It was now the three amigos! And life for Buddy and Linda continued to be richer than they ever could have imagined.

And one thing that no one could have ever imagined, was how Mark would actually assist them in raising their youngest son. But that is exactly what he did. Mark always loved taking care of Greg and was extremely gentle and protective of him. Buddy softly recalled Mark's love and affection for Greg sharing, "Mark used to love to hold Greg and would do most anything to get him to laugh. He would jump around and would love to play with him and his different toys."

Buddy continued, "Mark loved giving Greg his bottle and would even try giving his pacifier to him whenever he cried. Mark never liked to hear Greg cry." This sentiment was echoed, but also clarified, by Linda who added, "Mothers learn what the different cries of their children mean. But Mark thought it was urgent and that Greg was in pain anytime he cried. And he wanted me to get to him immediately!"

From the start it was easy to tell that Mark was special and his love for his brothers was something very unique. His natural instincts were to love and to protect his brothers, and to help them in any way that he could. He had an innate understanding of how to treat his brothers differently depending on the brother he was interacting with, and the situation in which they were interacting.

Linda explained, "He would get on the floor and play with Greg, but he didn't wrestle with him. He was a lot gentler with Greg than he was with Mike. With Mike, Mark was a follower. With Greg, Mark was a leader. However, she concluded, this would soon change as it wasn't long before Greg got as wild as both of his brothers!"

Linda credits Mike with how Mark interacted with his brothers. She lovingly reminisced how Mike had so much patience with Mark and how they would play together every day for hours at a time. She explained, "Mike taught Mark how to play every game he knew how to play. He also liked to act silly with him and make him laugh. The two loved to wrestle, and also watched cartoons together."

Linda smiled when she recalled how the two would imitate Batman when they were watching him on TV saying, "They each had Batman masks and capes that they would wear during the show. And they especially loved to act out the fight scenes. And although at times they loved to play rough, neither would ever cross the line or ever intentionally hurt the other."

Greg now had two willing teachers that continually shared with him all the things they themselves had already learned.
Likewise, Mike now had two students that he loved to teach and lead in whatever activities they would play. Mike would literally hold class for his brothers in the garage. He would stand in front

of the makeshift classroom using a chalkboard that Buddy had affixed to the wall. And Mark and Greg would act as the willing students attentively listening in old desks that gave the appearance and feel of actually being in a classroom.

This was a common activity that all the boys enjoyed. And while the topics discussed and the lessons learned are but memories that have long since faded, the joy these boys experienced on a daily basis just being together, is something that has continued throughout their adult lives

As the boys grew older, sports became an essential part of their lives. Mike being the oldest always seemed to set the path forward. Whether it was playing football, baseball, or basketball, Mike always had two brothers eager to compete with him whenever they had a free minute. The years spent in the back yard playing every sport imaginable was something that occupied nearly every day the weather would allow.

The games that were played ranged from tackle football, to basketball, to baseball, and even to home run derby. The last two sports were always played with a real baseball bat, but incorporated the use of a tennis ball for safety and for the protection of nearby windows. Of course, all of these games would include willing participants of some combination of friends and neighborhood kids. In the winter months you could always find this same group of kids sledding down Woodside Drive, which provided a nice hill right in front of the family home.

While the conventional sports were always fun, it was some of the more creative activities that have been most remembered. Such as the time Mark and Greg would hang from the mid-level second floor window with a pillow case in hand trying to master the art of parachuting. This required turning around and shimming out the window with their frontside towards the house and holding on to the window ledge before letting go and trying to inflate the pillow case before hitting the ground.

Linda recalls getting a call from a concerned neighbor who told her, "Linda I don't know if you are aware of this or not, but your boys are jumping out of the upstairs window." It was roughly a seven-foot drop to the ground which didn't seem like such a big deal at the time. After being busted following their third "successful jump", Linda promptly brought that activity to a screeching halt.

Another event the boys loved to do in the summer was called "Water Bogging." This was a homemade version of a popular attraction in which kids would sit or lay on a mat and would slide along a watery path down a hill into a wading pool. Having an inflatable swimming pool and a relatively large slide conveniently located in the back yard, they knew they had the makings of their very own water park. And by simply running a garden hose up the steps and tying it around the handle atop the slide, they had achieved the flow of water necessary to propel riders well past what a dry slide ever could. They then sweetened the deal by laying out thin deflated plastic rafts that were laid end to end, that would eventually carry the water bogger well into the neighbor's yard.

Anytime sports and water could be combined in any fashion, it was always going to be explored as a potential new activity the boys could enjoy. Whether it was running and sliding head first in the front yard after a good soaking rain, or simply tackling whoever had the football face down into a puddle, these were some of the best times the boys had playing in the yard.

Greg gave some context, saying, "The rain would always run along the edge of the front yard pooling just before the drive way. And we would line up to take a turn running down the yard launching ourselves head first, sliding several yards before splashing into the pooling pond of water that served as home plate."

Always having to take it up a notch, they soon took turns adding a catcher to the makeshift watery home plate who would pretend to try and tag out the would-be slider. Then it morphed into the other boys standing over the stream of water with their feet spread wide, as the runner now had to slide through the open legs of the other boys while making their way to the plate. And that is typically how these homemade games evolved, with the boys always finding a way to push the envelope in whatever they did.

Mark was especially fond of the tackle football games that were played throughout the year. Mark had become extremely strong and extremely determined, which made him hard to tackle. Mike vividly recalled, "Mark was always included in our pick-up football games as he had both great leg and upper body strength, which made him a good candidate to run the ball." Mike went on to say, "It took all of our effort to tackle him, so we never held back on doing what it took to get him to the ground!"

Mark concurred, saying, "I got no special treatment!" Mark affectionally summed it up this way, saying, "I loved to play football in the back yard with my brothers. They would tackle me in the muddy water. They would give me no special treatment. Now that was fun!"

These backyard sporting activities, both the conventional and the non-conventional ones, were played on what seemed to be a non-stop basis. And they seemed to somehow prepare all of the Hublar boys to excel in organized sports. The daily competitions also created a passion for winning that seemed to easily transfer to other areas of the boy's lives.

So, it wasn't long after Mike started to play on various sports teams that both Mark and Greg longed to do the same. And while they truly enjoyed watching their older brother play sports, a view from the sidelines was never going to be enough for these boys who couldn't wait to show others what they were made of as well.

The biggest takeaway from these early experiences of competition is the need to succeed that it seemingly fostered in the boys. And while for the most part, these contests stayed relatively friendly, some may have taken losing a little harder than others. Greg provided a view from the eyes of a younger brother, "Losing sucked! I hated losing back then. And truth be told, I'm not exactly fond of losing now!"

In any case, it was easy to see that the confidence and desire to compete that was alive and burning in Mark's brothers, was just as much alive and burning just as bright, in Mark. And soon it would be his turn to officially join the sports world!

First up for Mark would be playing baseball on the same team as Greg at the old Mt. Tabor Ballpark near Grant Line Road in New Albany. K U Heating and Cooling was a pewee team that both Mark and Greg played for simultaneously. It was typical of the league to try and keep brothers on the same team whenever possible for the convenience, and the sanity, of their parents.

While Mark was nearly four years older than Greg, no one really seemed to notice or give it a second thought. Mark was able to compete and to contribute to his baseball team, as his skill level was similar to that of his younger teammates. And Mark seemed to fit right in.

Next up for Mark was playing organized football for Our Lady of Perpetual Help. This was considered a deanery church team. So, the fact that Mark was attending a different school that provided classes for kids with special needs, it did not prevent him from participating. Again, he was able to join the team at the same time as Greg.

This particular team was designed for players in the fourth through sixth grade, which allowed Mark to easily blend in. Mark's smaller stature was never an issue. His strength and toughness, born of years of experience in the back yard, more than prepared him for the physical toughness demanded of each of the players.

Being able to be just like all of his brothers, and do all the same activities, has always been of the utmost importance to Mark. And when it came to sports, Mark was no different than any of his brothers!

As the boys continued to grow and became more involved in all types of activities, life for Buddy and Linda began to become very busy. Buddy continued to excel in his role as father and provider of the family. He enjoyed success working as a consultant to the business world, which involved periodic travel. And while many times this required long work days, he always enjoyed making time to attend any of his boys sporting events.

Meanwhile, Linda continued to excel in her role as a stay-at-home mom. She leaned heavily on her incredible organizational skills to keep everyone organized and on time. She credited her large monthly calendar, that hung just above the dryer in the laundry closet, as the key to her ability to successfully manage the schedules and activities of all the boys.

And everyday life, which at times had to be exhausting and certainly chaotic, but always full of love and excitement, soon became the new normal for this growing family of five!

But just as life seems to find its groove, or at least a rhythm that seems manageable, it has a unique way of changing when you least expect it. And in true real-world fashion, just as Buddy and Linda had settled into their most recent version of "Normal," life was about to change again.

Soon they discovered that a fourth child would be joining the gang towards the end of the year. And while four kids may seem to be more than most parent's today would care to handle, especially in light of how shall we say it, "the high energy level" of their first three children, the Lord saw fit to bless Buddy and Linda with yet another child.

If you are like many of Buddy and Linda's friends at the time, the thought of this couple finally having a daughter would bring a smile to your face. A gentle angel sent down from heaven to keep watch over the boys. One who could play quietly with dolls and bring a softening touch to an otherwise rough and tumble gang. A beautiful missing piece to round out the family. And a reprieve from the craziness.

Linda and Buddy's friends just knew this time around it was going to be a girl. So much so, that the baby shower that was thrown by one of their closest friends, Lou Ellen Endris, had a baby girl theme with all things pink! Afterall, a baby girl to round out this family of boys would parallel Linda's own birth.

However, if you really believe that this is what Buddy and Linda were hoping for at this point in their life, well then you haven't been paying enough attention to the story you have been reading.

Chapter 6: Where Is Everyone Going?

Mark was excited at the news of becoming an older brother again. He had already learned so much from both of his brothers. And he could hardly wait to teach what he had learned to this soon to be, newest addition to the family.

In the meantime, Mark continued to progress to unimaginable levels of achievement. He had far surpassed all medical, professional, and even social expectations, continuously leading his parents into uncharted territories. The truth of the matter is there was almost no written information, no progress charts to compare with, and certainly no road maps to follow concerning Down syndrome. It was still at a time when most of these precious children were unfortunately put into institutions shortly after birth, and sadly never heard from again.

However, Linda and Buddy remained steadfast in their determination to give Mark every opportunity that was afforded to his brothers. Linda recalled gaining inspiration from the movie "The Miracle Worker." This movie is based on the true story of Helen Keller. At nineteen months of age, Helen contracted what many believed was meningitis. This left her both blind and deaf.

Hellen is taught much more than just social graces by her teacher, Annie Sullivan. One scene in particular spoke directly to Linda's heart. It depicted Helen Keller walking around the dinner table taking food off of her family's plates with her hands and stuffing it in her mouth. This occurred as the family went on talking, as though nothing was wrong with it, as if it was perfectly normal behavior.

Linda recalled a particularly poignant line in which Annie Sullivan said "You train your dog how to behave. Why don't you do the same for your child?" Linda went on to reveal the impact that statement had on her, saying, "It really struck me just how important it was that Mark had to grow up with the same rules and manners as his brothers, and that we were not going to accept bad behavior from him just because he was born with Down syndrome." So, Buddy and Linda continued to treat Mark no differently than how they treated his brothers. This was especially true in public, and particularly in church, which could always be an adventure.

Buddy confirmed this stern approach, as he recalled one particular Sunday that didn't go exactly as planned. "We insisted that Mark kneel and sit at the proper times, and not turn around and look at the people behind him. We also required him not to talk in church, and that he paid attention to the alter and the priest. One day he was not following those rules and Linda turned around and pinched him on the leg to make him behave. Mark responded by screaming in a high pitch voice "SHE PINCHED ME!" Through his laughter, Buddy concluded the story by saying, "It seemed as though everyone in church turned around and looked at us. So, after church we scolded Mark for embarrassing us, and he never did it again!"

In hindsight, this firm but consistent approach, always wrapped in love, was key to not only Mark's maturation, but also the foundation of how his brothers would treat him. Since he was treated like the rest of his siblings, including being required to live up to his responsibilities, doing his chores, receiving discipline, having to go to school, obey the rules, etc., there was really no reason, or even opportunity, to see him as any different. At least not through the eyes of his brothers.

Mike gave his first-hand perspective, saying, "It would be many years later before I realized that Mark was different from me. I never felt obligated to treat him special and therefore I felt no resentment or jealousy towards him or our relationship. He was just my younger brother who happened to have an extra chromosome."

While Mike began to branch out on his own, attending pre-school and then kindergarten, Greg and Mark began spending more and more time together. Every day they talked and played together. However, Mark always had trouble pronouncing his S's, as the sound came out of the side of his mouth instead of the front. A trait his younger brother apparently picked up on. And as a result, both he and Greg had to go to speech therapy to learn how to pronounce their words correctly. Even so, at times it was difficult to understand what Mark was saying. But Greg always knew what he was trying to say and he would translate it for anyone struggling to understand.

Linda distinctly recalled one thing that always threw her for a loop. She explained, "Every night when I kissed Mark goodnight, he would fold his hands like he was saying a prayer, bow his head, and say a word that I couldn't understand. So, I finally asked Greg if he knew what Mark was saying. Greg said, "Oh sure, he's saying Sayonara (sigh a Nora)." He went on to tell me how the two of them would always watch a cartoon about a little Japanese mouse. And how at the end of the show, the mouse would bow and say sayonara, which means goodbye."

Greg served as Mark's impromptu interpreter while he was learning to speak clearly. Linda recalls how frustrated Greg would get when she was trying to get Mark to use his words instead of just pointing and grunting. She explained, "Instead of telling me what he wanted, Mark would point or make gestures. Greg always knew what he wanted. However, the doctor told me to act like I didn't understand what Mark wanted in hopes of making him try and say the word." Linda went on to say, "This almost drove Greg crazy. And even though he was used to translating for me, I had to pretend like I didn't understand, until Mark attempted to say the word. After Greg realized what I was doing, it became easier for him to let the process play out. And as a result, Mark began using his words instead of gestures."

Soon it was time to welcome the newest member into the Hublar family. And on November 2, 1974, Todd Christopher Hublar was born healthy and strong. A welcome addition, he arrived as the fourth and final son born into this family. Life was in full swing as Mike was now eleven years old, Mark was ten, and Greg was six.

Both Mike and Greg were full time students at Our Lady of Perpetual Help. Both had established their own friends and both were playing sports. Mark was enrolled in a special education class at St. Mary of the Knobs where he was one of eight students. However, the school did not have a sports program of any kind. So according to Linda, "Todd was a life saver for Mark."

Mark has always enjoyed being around his brothers. Even to this day, Mark gets excited at any opportunity to spend time with his brothers. So, it was no surprise that with Greg now beginning to branch out into his own young life, Mark was thrilled to once again have someone to play with and to teach new things.

Buddy recalled how proud he was of Mark and how he had become such a wonderful older brother, saying, "Mark was now older, and he could teach Todd so much more than he taught Greg. By that time, he was able to talk much clearer, and was able to do so many more things." Mark was always ready and willing to help any of his brothers. And he looked forward to continuing to teach Todd everything that he himself had learned!"

Mark continued the tradition of playing school with the old school desks and the large blackboard that still hung on the wall in the garage. This time around Mark would be the teacher, with Todd being the willing student. Together they had workbooks with lots of math problems, spelling words, colors and shapes. And as the years went by, Mark continued to spend a growing amount of his time with Todd.

However, Todd also spent a fair amount of time with all of his brothers growing up. So, it didn't take Todd very long before he started catching up with Mark. And soon, they started to learn from each other. And as Todd grew older, he was very patient with Mark, and still let Mark be the teacher. The friendship that had blossomed over the years between Todd and Mark became all the more important, as both Mike and Greg became more engaged in their own social life, and had found themselves spending less and less time at home.

The days continued to pass and the boys continued to grow. And something new began happening in New Albany. It was called Inclusion. Public schools now were offering special education classes for children with any form of disability. Buddy and Linda were advised to enroll Mark into these classes as they would give him a path to continue his education. They were told if it didn't work out, he could always go back to school at St. Mary of the Knobs.

Linda recalled feeling somewhat apprehensive at the idea of Mark leaving the security of his small school for a seemingly gigantic public school. She said, "My meeting with the principal made me feel a little bit better. He told me that 98% of the students were good kids and would be kind to Mark, but 2% of them "belong behind bars." Linda emphasized, "Those were his words, not mine." So, Mark and his parents took a leap of faith and he began attending classes at Hazelwood Jr High. Linda later remarked, "He ended up having wonderful teachers. And he felt like for the first time he was in a "normal" school, just like his brothers!"

Mark loved being around so many other students as he thrived in this new environment. On the academic side, he was doing great, making the A-B Honor Roll nearly every semester. However, on the sports side, not so much, as the school sports programs seemed to be a little out of his reach.

Linda somberly recalled, "He tried out for the football team, but most of the kids were already so much bigger than Mark. The coach at the time was our long-time friend, Chizzie Wolf. Understanding the situation, he offered Mark a position as the official water boy which would allow him to sit on the bench and be considered part of the team, without the risk of getting hurt."

She continued, "And in baseball, his age group had switched to fast pitch which also made it hard for Mark to be competitive. So, that sport ended for him as well." She concluded, "And the basketball team had a height requirement of 5'5", so basketball would only be happening in pick-up games, mostly with his brothers."

However, not all was lost. Determined to find a sport in which Mark could participate, Buddy and Linda suggested he try out for the Hazelwood wrestling team. After watching endless hours of professional wrestling on TV, and getting lots of real-life practice with his three brothers over the years, it seemed logical that Mark would be a natural. And low and behold, he was.

Mark was welcomed on to the wrestling team and was now once again, "just like his brothers!" In wrestling, you compete against other wrestlers within your own weight classification. And Mark has always been extremely strong for his size. Soon, Mark began winning blue ribbons. And now he too had things to put on his trophy shelf, just like his brothers!

Although Mark was progressing very nicely with his own life, and was truly a success beyond all measures, the thing that he has always treasured the most was quickly fading away. And that was the seemingly endless days of spending time with all of his brothers.

Through no fault of anyone, life waits for no one. And life was definitely changing for Mark. While he still enjoyed hanging out with Todd, the times that all four boys were available at the same time became less and less. Sports, friends, school activities, and even girlfriends, all became the focus of attention for Mark's brothers.

Gone were the days when starting a pickup game in the back yard was as easy as yelling up the stairs, and then putting on your shoes. So too, gone were the days of family room wrestling matches, indoor nerf hoops, somersaults off the headboard onto Mom and Dad's bed, and the fearless jumps out of the upstairs window.

Even the air hockey games, in which Mike would challenge his dad, while his three brothers cheered, soon became a distant memory. This one was especially fun knowing that a pizza waited for the boys, if Mike could take down his old man. Looking back, it was a good thing that Buddy liked pizza too. Otherwise, who knows how many games Mike really would have won?

In any case, life was definitely changing for the boys, and Mark was there to witness it all. And to say he was not a fan of the changes, would be a great understatement!

Chapter 7: Time To Move On

Before we move forward, it is worth taking a look back to see just how far Mark had actually come to arrive at this point in his life. Early along the way, Mark attended school at the Rauch Center. The Rauch Center was actually the first school for children with developmental disabilities in the state of Indiana. Its humble beginnings can be traced back to a grassroots effort to fill a need that was going overlooked.

Mrs. Leona Receveur was a determined lady who had a daughter with Down syndrome that was not allowed to attend public school. As a result, she began contacting other parents who were facing the same problem. And in 1953, joined by a group of dedicated parents, they became the catalyst for special programming that began in a church basement with a volunteer teacher. But it wasn't long before this organization found the financial support that it needed as it became the first entity in Southern Indiana to be funded by the WHAS Crusade for Children.

WHAS is the local affiliate of the American Broadcasting Company (ABC). And the WHAS Crusade for Children is an agency whose stated mission is: "To make life better for children with special needs by inspiring generosity with our community partners." Rabbi Joseph Rauch, an original Crusade panelist, was instrumental in helping Rauch obtain funding in 1958 for its Charlestown Road site, which is located in New Albany, Indiana. Today, Rauch Inc directly serves over 1,000 children, adults, and families from five sites. Counties serviced in Indiana include Clark, Floyd, Harrison, Jackson, Jefferson, Scott, and Washington.

In its first sixty-six years of existence, the Crusade for Children raised more than $190 million, with 100% of those donations going towards children with special needs. The annual fundraising event is televised each year on a weekend in June. This event holds a special memory for Mark, as it is here that he made his television debut as an 11-year-old back in 1975. This in turn led to an article featuring Mark and his involvement with the Crusade for Children. It appeared in the Courier Journal, which is the primary newspaper serving Louisville and Southern Indiana residents. Little did anyone know at the time, that a star was being born!

Mark's formal education began at the Rauch Center, which is still in existence today. Their vision continues to imagine a community where everyone belongs, and believes everyone should enjoy a sense of contribution, value and self-worth. Linda gratefully recalled, "It was the only school of its kind in this area. And it was a wonderful experience!" Mark would attend school at the Rauch Center for four years. But soon it would be time for him to take his next big step.

Margie Stemle, who happened to be Mark's aunt, worked as a teacher's aide at St Mary of the Knobs School in Floyd's Knobs, Indiana. She had told Buddy and Linda about the wonderful special education class that she was teaching, and how much the students were learning. Convinced this would be a nice opportunity for Mark, they signed him up to begin classes at the beginning of the next school year.

His classroom contained eight students, two teacher's aids, and the primary teacher, Sister Mary Patrick. The students were taught math, word pronunciation, typing, sewing, piano, and most importantly, reading.

Mark one day being able to read was a dream of Buddy and Linda's. One they faithfully prayed would come true. And even though it was now part of Mark's school curriculum, they were not prepared when it actually began to happen.

Linda explained, "One night we were helping Mark with his homework, and we thought he was just repeating something he had memorized. But then his dad and I realized he was actually reading. Neither one of us could contain our tears." She continued, "I wrote a note to Sister Mary Patrick thanking her and calling her our very own "Miracle Worker." I found out later that she had kept that note and asked for our permission to print it in a newsletter at her convent."

From there, Mark then made the leap into mainstream schooling starting with special education classes at Hazelwood Middle School. Going to Hazelwood gave Mark an even higher level of confidence as he was now going to a mainstream school just like all of his brothers. A constant theme in Mark's life has always been his desire to be just like his brothers. His proudest statement to this day is being able to tell anyone who will listen that "I am just like my brothers."

Getting up every day to an alarm clock, getting himself ready for school, coming home and doing his homework, and laying out his clothes for the next day definitely gave him the opportunity to be just like his brothers. In truth, he was actually more organized, and definitely more dedicated to school, than any of his brothers at the time.

These four years at Hazelwood, were followed by three more years of continuing special education classes at New Albany High School. Mark loved everything about high school, including the classes, the teachers, working in the cafeteria, the talent shows, the ball games, and the proms. To this day, Mark continues to attend each of his high school reunions. One of his favorite memories is winning the coveted title of being "Mr. Red and Black." This was a title reserved for being the person voted on as having the most school spirit.

This particular vote occurred at a pep session in front of the entire school. The outcome was determined by the volume of applause one would receive when the name of a candidate was announced. While no doubt some people may have voted in jest, the overwhelming people in that school who knew Mark, loved him. This is evident by the people that still stop him just to say hello. It's amazing how Mark never forgets anyone, and very rarely forgets a name!

One of Mark's pride and joys from that time in his life is his high school class ring. It has a blue birthstone, and it displays the school emblem, his graduation date, and the image of a wrestler on it. He still wears it with pride each and every day.

However, by this time in Mark's life, Mike and Greg were spending even less time at home, and more time pursuing their individual goals. This provided an opportunity for Mark and Todd to spend more time together, which ultimately strengthened their bond even more than before. But just because they were spending so much time together, didn't mean the games they would play were any less competitive. One trait that is true of all the Hublar boys is a desire to win at whatever the task at hand may be.

Case in point was on one particular vacation in which Mark and Todd, along with Buddy and Linda, were traveling to the east coast. They made a stop at a theme park in New York to ride the Alpine Slide. This attraction featured two lanes of essentially concrete, in which a rider would sit in a cart, one in each lane, and would race down the hill simultaneously in an attempt to cross the finish line first.

Todd remembered it well, saying, "Mark and I raced down the hill, one of us on each side. We were both flying down the hill trying to reach the finish line first. When we got close to the finish line, Mark's cart completely flipped over and he slid face first on the concrete!" Buddy happened to be videotaping the race and captured the whole thing. Fortunately, Mark was not hurt, well not by the "Hublar standard" anyway.

Thinking back on watching that video, Todd remarked, "The thing that still sticks with me today is that after he crashed, Mark got up as quick as he could, flipped his cart back over, and jumped in it as fast as he could to try to catch me." Todd went on to say, "It was a nasty crash, yet Mark never stopped to worry about his scrapes and bruises. And he never gave up." Todd affectionately concluded, "I think that kind of summarizes how Mark lives his life. He doesn't find excuses to quit. And he always wants to do the best that he can, no matter what challenges he faces."

Mark's life has never been one in which the outcome of a particular quest was ever a certainty. Not by any stretch of the imagination. But Buddy and Linda have always kept their promise to God to allow Mark to go as far as he was capable of going. Their faith and confidence in Mark's ability have been fueled over the years, all the more, by the many milestones that Mark has surpassed. And in most cases, far surpassed.

However, when Buddy talks about giving his sons the freedom to fail, sometimes that is exactly what happens. Buddy reinforced his belief, saying, "The key is being there to pick them up when they do fail. And then having the courage to allow them to try it again." This belief shared by both Buddy and Linda, demonstrated in how they raised all four of their sons, was put to the test in a mighty way.

Mark has always been allowed to try virtually anything his brothers were allowed to do. This included everything from riding bicycles on the street, to motorbikes in the yard. So, when Mark asked to ride Greg's moped around the block, it didn't seem like such a big deal.

Mark had proven his ability to ride an off-road motorbike years before. And he regularly rode his bicycle on the streets to the local swimming pool, as well as to a lot of different places. However, this day it would be different. This day would be one that would never be forgotten.

Mark was allowed to ride the moped around the block. Back then, helmets were not required. And they certainly were not considered cool. So, without one, Mark confidently drove off around the corner and out of view. Minutes later a neighbor would be frantically knocking on the door, informing Linda that Mark had been hit by a car on Klerner Lane.

Upon arriving at the scene, Mark was laying in the middle of the road unconscious and feared dead. Linda recounted that awful sight saying, "Mark was lying in the middle of the road with his eyes wide open, but totally unconscious. I thought for sure he was dead." She continued, "The unfortunate lady that hit Mark must of thought he was dead as well, as she went into shock and had to be taken by ambulance to the hospital".

Fortunately, Mark recovered in the hospital from a severe concussion, but no broken bones or any other severe injuries.

And within a few days, both Mark and the other driver had been released from the hospital and were recovering at home.

As for the moped, that was a different story. The gas tank, which was positioned under the handle bars and running vertically down to the footboard, was dented from what appeared to be contact with Mark's knee as he went airborne before landing in the sprawled out, unconscious position, in which he was found.

To say it would take both faith and courage to ever allow Mark on a moped again would be a great understatement. And a story for another chapter. However, this challenge was only a foreshadowing of a challenge that would require even more faith, and even more courage.

To say there were not ups and downs, successes and failures, and questions as to whether Buddy and Linda were on track, or off their rocker when it came to what they were willing to allow Mark to try, well I guess that is up to you, the reader, to decide. But as far as Buddy and Linda were concerned, they would continue to rely heavily on their faith, and on their unwavering belief that all of their sons deserved the opportunity to reach their full God-given potential.

They never allowed the inevitable stares, whispers, and misguided comments, and even the occasional well-intentioned but often bad advice, to ever stop them from living out what they believed was the right way to raise their family. And with each passing day, that resolve, that confidence, that loving acceptance was being instilled into all four of their sons, who were quickly turning into men.

A line from a particular country song mentions how the days go slow but the years go fast. And I guess that sentiment could apply to most families, as it certainly applied to this family. Mike had now long since left for college and would soon be graduating from Indiana University and moving to Kokomo, Indiana to begin his career. Shortly after that, he would marry Debra, the love of his life and high school sweetheart. Linda recalled, "That was the first big hit for Mark."

Soon after, Greg would also be leaving the nest to attend Indiana University. Greg not only earned a degree, but also met the love of his life along the way. And He and Lisa would be married just four months after graduating in 1990. Linda added, "That was the second hit for Mark."

Not long after that, Todd would follow in both Mike and Greg's footsteps in playing football for Our Lady of Providence High School. He too would have the honor and privilege of playing for Hall of Fame Coach Gene Sartini. This understandably took up a large majority of Todd's time. Linda sadly concluded, "That was the third and final hit for Mark, as he no longer had any of his brothers in which to hang out with anymore."

Times had obviously changed. And now the ability for Mark to continue to be "just like his brothers," seemed to be slipping away. Linda tried to frame Mark's new situation in a positive light as she explained, "Mark stayed busy working at Ace Remanufacture, a company in which his father was a co-owner. He also began playing sports with the Special Olympics. He was a member of the Special Friends Club, so he had a very busy life as well." However, she couldn't gloss over the fact that for the most part, the only people at home for Mark to hang out with were his parents.

Understandably, Mark began spending a lot more time alone in his room. He did however have his own TV, as well as his own phone line. He was able to pay for the separate line with the money he was making from working at Ace Remanufacture.

Linda opened up a little more, sharing, "Mark didn't expect us to entertain him. He loved to read and write stories. He enjoyed many shows on TV, especially wrestling. I prepared all of his meals, did his laundry, and provided his transportation. So, I thought life was pretty good for him." "However," she added, "He did have to follow house rules which included no loud music, lights out when we went to bed, and he had to keep his drum set in the garage."

Mark was now twenty-four years old, and a man by all accounts. Linda and Buddy had long since known how blessed they would be to see the day he could reasonably take care of himself. They had always believed that Mark living with them, until either he or they would die, would always just be part of the deal. They were not only prepared for this, but regularly thanked God for Buddy's answered prayer; that of Mark one day being able to love and serve the Lord!

What more could they have possibly asked for? Mark was more than reasonably self-sufficient. He was making his own money. He was hanging out in his own "bachelor pad" of a room. He had full control of his own television, and his own phone line that he didn't have to hand over if a call came in for his parents. By all accounts he seemed to be living the dream.

However, as much of a miracle as Mark's life had already turned out to be, there was one concern that was understandably being overlooked by everyone, except Mark. And that was Mark's never-ending, white hot, burning desire to be just like his brothers. And when Mark says that he wants to be "Just Like My Brothers," it is not just a mantra, or some type of cliché. But rather invokes a seriousness more along the lines of Patrick Henry's quote from his 1775 speech to the Second Virginia Convention in which he is credited with saying "Give me liberty or give me death".

And much to Buddy and Linda's bewilderment, Mark approached them both informing them that it was now time for him to move on!

Chapter 8: Unimaginable Blessings

Buddy and Linda's love for Mark, as well as for all their sons, knows no bounds. And from the very beginning, they had simply accepted the fact that Mark would always live with them. Buddy, in a very sincere but matter of fact way said, "We just accepted that he would be living with us forever. We never even gave it a second thought."

Buddy went on to say, "It was our decision to keep Mark out of an institution, and to help him become everything that he possibly could be. Furthermore, we have always been committed to not burdening anyone, especially his brothers, with our decision."

Buddy concluded, "Linda and I have always been committed to accepting any life disruptions and sacrifice that our decision would require us to undergo". Linda remembered it the very same way, "We always expected Mark to live with us forever. We just thought that was the way it worked."

Being basically the last of the Hublar boys in the nest, Mark continued to spend much of his time entertaining himself. He enjoyed watching television, watching movies on his VCR (Video Cassette Recorder for the younger readers), watching professional wrestling, listening to music, and playing on his drums. The latter was not one of his parent's favorite activities as the noise would vibrate throughout the house.

Mark also spent a lot of time with a book opened and would write word for word everything that was written in the book. Buddy remarked, "Although Mark really did not understand what he was writing, he loved to write and work at his desk. I think this was his way of being like his brothers."

Linda somberly reflected back, "I knew it couldn't be much fun for him having to live with his parents. We weren't that old, but we didn't have the energy to keep up with a guy in his twenties. And we certainly didn't have the love for loud music, nor wrestling matches, that he did."

However, not even Buddy nor Linda could quite comprehend the depths of how much Mark sorely missed having his brothers around. The seemingly endless days of always having someone to hang out with, had somehow, sadly come to an end. No more were the days of backyard sports, sliding in the rain, wrestling matches in the family room, family vacations with all his brothers, or even someone to spend rainy days with cooped up in the house.

Although Mark's youngest brother was still living at home at the time, Todd was now preparing to enter high school. And his life had understandably become busy with sports, school activities, and the type of active social life that kept him on the go. As we all know, time slows down for no one. And this would be the next lesson that Mark would not only learn, but would soon be teaching to his parents.

By now you should be able to understand, or at least recognize the fact, that Mark has always had a burning desire to be just like his brothers. However, one thing that you may not know about Mark is that he strongly believed that he should be the next in line after Mike, to do anything that Mike did. And It bothered him deeply when one of his younger brothers surpassed him.

It didn't matter if it was getting a driver's license, having a girlfriend, going to college, getting married, or even just moving out of the house. For Mark, there was definitely an order as to how things were supposed to happen. And when it didn't, Mark would do everything he could to make things right.

This typically meant he would begin working on a solution that would ensure he didn't fall behind. Mark has always needed order and structure in his life. And that included keeping the hierarchy of the Hublar boys intact!

Mike, the oldest of all the brothers, shared his perspective, "It always seemed like it was such a joyous occasion when I would reach one of life's milestones, such as getting a driver's license, going to college, or getting married. Mark and my family were always so supportive. And it seemed to give Mark a glimpse of things he had to look forward to." "Looking back," Mike said, "I think Mark expected me to go first and lead the way. However, it did not always sit well with him when one of our younger brothers experienced some of these same milestones ahead of him!"

Mike continued, "Mark always seemed to struggle during these times, as it may have made him aware of some of the challenges he was facing as a normal person with Down syndrome." He concluded, "Mark has always considered himself "normal" and to this day Mark believes that he still must tell people that he has Down syndrome because he honestly doesn't think they can tell from just talking to him."

Speaking of "normal," Mark's version of it certainly didn't involve him sticking around home waiting for his last brother to leave the nest before him. Staying home with his mom and dad for the rest of his life may have been a part of Buddy and Linda's plan. But little did they know, it was definitely not part of Mark's plan!

Reflecting back, Linda searched for clues that might have indicated Mark's growing desire for independence at the time. One thought quickly came to her mind, "Greg invited Mark to stay with him on several weekends at IU, and they went to some parties together. I believe that's when the seeds were planted for him to live on his own and be his own boss."

Greg chimed in: "Those were some good times! And I loved showing Mark what the IU experience was all about. From having no curfew, to attending keg parties, to things we won't talk about here, Mark was my brother and I never gave it a second thought."

God has always had a plan for Mark's life, as he does for all of our lives, including yours! And like most of God's really big plans, this particular plan for the next phase of Mark's life, was a little hard to fathom.

Mark was already a miracle by anyone's standard. The odds that he had defied throughout his life, simply boggle the mind. But when he approached Buddy and Linda at the age of twenty-four, informing them it was now time for him to leave home, there were no words that could begin to describe the thoughts and emotions that had just been triggered in the hearts and minds of his parents.

Linda tried to put it into context, "We were completely blindsided! He had never mentioned it before and we had never thought of it even being a possibility!" Al agreed, saying, "We didn't even know he was thinking about it, so we never saw it coming. But, since we pushed him to always stand on his own, I guess we shouldn't have been so surprised."

Linda remembered the truly mixed emotions she had upon hearing Mark's declaration. She tried to explain it this way, "I was happy that he was so normal, and that he wanted what most guys his age wanted. But I was also petrified that he wasn't prepared. A million things went through my head telling me why it was a bad idea. My first thought was to ask him to wait until he was older."

But after a brief pause, she provided even more insight to the challenge that was now before them by rhetorically asking, "But at what age would a young man with Down syndrome be old enough to move out of his family home and live on his own? Would we make our other sons wait? Would we hold them back, or would we encourage them and try to support their decision?"

She concluded by emphatically saying, "We knew the answers to those questions immediately!" Buddy thoughtfully added, "We were concerned, but we knew that Mark had to make his own decisions. And that we had no right to stop him from trying to achieve anything he wanted to accomplish!"

Linda recalled hoping that a group home could be a possible solution. When the first group home moved into New Albany, she took a part time job there just to see how it all worked. She recalls one particular Saturday that she brought Mark over to rake leaves, eat lunch, and meet the guys that lived there. And when they got home, she asked Mark if he thought he would like living in a group home.

But Mark hated the idea. Mainly because he would have a roommate that would have to sleep in the same room. Not to mention he would still have to follow other people's rules, and thus not truly being as independent as he longed to be. And Mark simply would have no part of that. He wanted to live in his own place, with his own rules. In short, he wanted to be just like his brothers.

Buddy and Linda were once again at a crossroads. Would they do the prudent thing that most people expected out of them, including their own parents. Or would they somehow muster up the faith and understanding that Mark living on his own was actually a part of the Lord's will. Linda seemingly went back in time to revisit the struggle that she and Buddy went through in order to provide some type of perspective.

She then shared the following, "Raising Mark has always been a challenge of trying to do the right thing. Some of the things we let him do were unconventional. But Mark was so determined to be like his brothers that no matter what the challenge, we had to give him the chance. All we could do was try to follow our other son's examples, and to trust in Mark's courage and determination." She concluded, "His brothers survived, and we felt Mark would too. We put a lot of trust in God that He would guide us to make the right decision."

Linda shared even more insight as to what actually went into their decision-making process, "We were willing to give Mark the chance, and what other people thought really didn't matter to us. We had a lot of self-doubt. We even asked ourselves if we were absolutely crazy to let him try to live on his own, as it was completely unheard of at the time. Were we the worst parents in the world? Would this turn out to be a good or bad idea? We both have a very strong faith in God. And we feel like He has guided us every step of the way raising our four sons, and that He wouldn't fail us now."

Al, looking back on their decision to allow Mark the chance to live on his own, gave a glimpse into some of the resistance they were feeling. He explained, "Most people couldn't believe what we were allowing Mark to do. Even our own parents were concerned about our decision. But we never had a role model to follow. Nor did we have any sound advice available from any professionals like there is now. We just had one goal – to help Mark reach his full potential, wherever that would lead him!"

The decision to give Mark a chance to live on his own had now been made. Mark would get the opportunity he so deeply wanted. There is a saying that describes the hand of God when he calls one to a mission. That being: "God doesn't call the equipped, but rather, He equips the called." And that would seem to apply quite nicely to this particular situation, as a one-bedroom house had just gone up for rent on Klerner Lane, which was very close to their home. More evidence that seemed to support that this was in fact the Lord's will began to surface, as the owner of the house was willing to allow Mark to try living there for a couple of days, without signing a long-term lease.

But even though it was easy to get caught up in the incredible excitement of Mark actually getting the chance to live on his own, to say there were no reservations and concerns would not be honest. Buddy gave a glimpse into the doubt that they both fought so hard to keep at bay, "We thought it would last a few days or until he got lonely, or hungry, or both. But were we ever wrong!"

The day had finally arrived and Mark moved into his new bachelor pad. Buddy installed a deadbolt on the front door, which was the only entry door to the house. He then installed three smoke detectors, covering every square inch of the house. Linda helped Mark unpack, and generally tried to get his things organized.

However, Mark had already known that one of the best parts of living on his own would be doing things his way. And that included arranging his furniture, and decorating his walls, with things he liked. Linda quickly realized that it was truly time for her to start loosening the reins. The resulting layout was vintage Mark Hublar!

As you walked through the front door, there sat his full set of drums in his "music room", with pictures of Elvis on the walls. The next room was his TV Room, which had pictures of his favorite wrestlers on all the walls. In his bedroom, he had a large picture of Jesus and a crucifix. Mark also had many family photos lovingly displayed around the house. For security reasons, Mark would bring his moped inside and park it on a large heavy piece of plastic in his music room.

Mark had now clearly spread his wings and proudly soared to the same level of independence that he had seen his brothers achieve. But would it last?

Linda admittedly struggled with the new living arrangements, but noted Mark made the adjustment very quickly. "That first week, I was at his house every day; cooking, organizing, and making lists of things he needed." So much so, Linda recalled Buddy having to remind her that it was Mark's house, and that she didn't live there. He told her, "Be happy for him and quit smothering him, give him his space."

However, Linda confided that it was hard for her to believe that Mark could actually survive on his own. But Mark absolutely loved living on his own. And even though he lived only a couple of blocks away, he didn't come home even once that first week.

Even Buddy, who has always believed there was nothing that any of his sons couldn't achieve, was amazed at Mark's independence. "I was surprised that he didn't come back, or even visit us as often as we thought. I guess He was just being like his brothers."

Life was good for Mark as he would frequently play his drums as loud, and as often, as he wanted. He loved being able to play his music whenever he wanted, and as loud as he wanted. Mark also had a very active social life at the time. Thanks in part to Kathy Wilkerson, who organized the Special Friends Club and planned many events. These events included such things as bowling, pizza parties, movies, wrestling matches, once a year mystery trips, which were overnight trips to places like Gun Smoke Mountain, Spring Mill, as well as attending out of town ball games.

Mark played on every Special Olympics team that the New Albany Parks Department offered, including track and field, bowling, softball, and basketball. Mark was living the kind of life that twenty-four years earlier, no one could have imagined!

However, Mark was not living on a free ride by any stretch. Just like his brothers, he was working 40 hours a week. He drove his moped each day to Ace Remanufacture, where he worked in an unairconditioned plant as a custodian, as well as an automotive parts cleaner. He paid his own rent, bought his own groceries, and covered virtually all of his other expenses with his own money. During the warm months, he also rode his moped wherever he needed or wanted to go, including church.

When he was home, wrestling was Mark's favorite thing to watch on TV. He also enjoyed watching "Saved by the Bell," "Full House," and "Little House on the Prairie." Usually, one night a week on the weekends, he would pop popcorn and enjoy his own "movie night." By all accounts, his life didn't look a whole lot different from the average Non-Down syndrome American Bachelor!

Mark has always been very neat and clean, and has found security in being organized and on time. Some of his first purchases for his new place were a vacuum sweeper, broom, mop, furniture polish, and window cleaner.

In the beginning, Mark would prepare his own breakfast and lunch, while Linda would bring his dinner to him. Typically, these were meals that could be heated in the microwave. Linda proudly recounted Mark's progress in the kitchen, "Mark had used the microwave and stove, and even the oven, while he was still living with us. But he had never prepared a full meal. But after just the second week, he asked me to type out some of his favorite recipes, such as chili, meatloaf, Shake and Bake pork chops and Shake and Bake chicken. He put the recipes in a notebook that he called his "Cookbook." And from that point on, he began preparing his own meals!"

She added, "Mark, even began doing his own laundry!" Although that would require a quick trip back to his parent's house in order to use their washer and dryer.

Weeks quickly turned into months, and months turned into years. It became evident that this was not a phase, or some type of stunt that was going to run its course before returning to the tranquility and safety of the way things used to be. Mark absolutely loved his independence. And he was proud to tell people, "I live on my own, in my own house." He loved being his own boss and making his own rules. His self-confidence was very high, as he knew he was now on par with his brothers. Living on his own was everything he hoped it would be.

Mark really enjoyed when his friends would stop by for a visit. However, he didn't want his house to become a hang out, nor did he want any visitor to disrespect his place. So, he wrote out a list of "House Rules" and taped them on the wall next to his front door. These were rules that I am confident we all have, even if we're not so bold as to post them for all to see. They simply included: "No Smoking." "No Drinking." "No Cussing." "No Tearing Up My House."

Once in a while Mark complained of being lonely. But anytime Buddy and Linda suggested getting a roommate, his response was always the same: "No roommate, I want to save the extra space for my wife!"

To say there were not some growing pains, as well as some bumps in the road as Mark learned how to truly live on his own, would not be telling the full story. Mark and his parents had to learn how to mutually respect each other's privacy. Linda made sure to start calling before she stopped by. And she began to cut her visits way back. Mark, for his part, committed to not calling them on the phone every time he thought of something. It seemed to work out well as Mark learned to write his thoughts on paper, and then share them with his parents during his daily phone call. He knew that if something was an emergency, he could call them anytime.

Linda pondered on that unique time of transition and confessed, "My mistake was worrying too much. It was just so easy to think about all the bad things that could happen." She went deeper into her confession, saying, "At first, I didn't have enough faith in Mark. But I soon learned that he was very capable, and was able to do everything that needed to be done."

However, some of the fears that Linda had, turned out to be legitimate. As in the case when a couple of underage boys that Mark new from the neighborhood took advantage of him living on his own. They weren't particularly mean kids, but saw an opportunity and took advantage of it. The boys were not old enough to buy beer, so they came over to Mark's house and asked him to buy it for them. So, he did. Linda recalled the disappointing occurrence, saying, "Mark told us about it the next day. All we had to do was tell him he could go to jail for buying beer for minors, and he never did it again." Lesson learned.

And there was that stretch of time where Mark had a hard time staying awake at work. This was unusual for Mark, as he had always gone to bed on time and got up on his own with no problem. So, for him to suddenly not be able to complete an eight-hour shift without falling asleep became a real mystery.

Until one day Buddy and Mark were out shopping, and in a chance encounter, a man walked up to Mark and gave him a big hug. He said he had missed seeing Mark at a local night club that remained open until 2:00am during the week. It turned out this gentleman was the owner of a local establishment who genuinely enjoyed Mark visiting his club.

From time to time, he would even allow Mark to get on the stage and sing with the band. And even though Mark didn't drink, and it was only a couple of blocks from his house, they always made sure to give him a ride home when the bar closed. Fortunately for Mark, this revelation came several years after the fact, and long after that phase had passed!

Mark lived by himself on Klerner Lane for eight years. He had changed jobs a couple of times over that period, but always made enough money to support himself. He continued to become more self-sufficient. And his moped continued to get him to most places that he needed or wanted to go. In all that time, he never moved back home except for a short period, when he was recovering from shoulder surgery. But even then, after just a week of living with his parents, he once again informed them that it was time for him to go back home.

The fear and doubt that had existed in the early days of Mark living on his own, were but a distant memory. Mark had once again shocked the world, and shifted society's paradigm of what someone with Down syndrome was actually capable of accomplishing, when given a chance. Mark knew that no one could say that he was not just like his brothers. And nothing made him happier than that!

It seemed like Mark would live on Klerner Lane for the rest of his life. He obviously loved it, and everything was continuing to work out well. However, little did anyone know, God was only getting warmed up with His plan for Mark's life. And while Buddy and Linda's life seemed to have found its next nice groove, Joe Stemle, Linda's loving father, was starting to lose his.

"On two different occasions, we came to Dad's house and found him on the floor," Linda sadly recalled. Joe had a mini-stroke both times. He was still living on his own, in the home that Linda had actually grown up in. He refused to move into a nursing home. But it became apparent that it wasn't safe for him to be alone.

Linda recalled that stressful period in her life, "At that time I was working for the Parks Department in order to help pay for Todd's college. So, I couldn't spend a lot of time with him." However, she did cook his meals and managed to visit him every day. But she felt he needed more. So, she began praying and working on a plan.

Mark obviously loves his independence. He worked hard to not only achieve it, but to maintain it. However, one thing that Mark has always loved more than even his independence, is his family. Whether it be an immediate family member, a cousin, a niece or a nephew, Mark never forgets a birthday. The love he shows the world originates with his God, and transfers to his family.

So, when Linda asked Mark if he would be interested in moving into his Grandfather's house in order to help him, he immediately said yes. Excitedly, Linda said, "Mark was happy about the move and sincerely wanted to help his Grandpa!" And Joe liked the idea of having someone in the house with him. He thought having a grandson there was a lot better than hiring a stranger to help take care of him. Joe definitely did not like the thought of a nursing home, and would only refer to it as "Plan B."

Now, before you start thinking this was simply going to be a match made in heaven, you have to remember that these were a couple of bachelors that had become accustomed to doing things their own way. There would obviously need to be some compromises and adjustments, if this arrangement was actually going to work.

But they each had their own space, along with their own phone line and TV. Mark maintained his primary residence upstairs, while his Grandpa lived on the main floor. In addition, his Grandpa's phone was programmed so all he had to do was press #1 on his phone, and it would ring Mark's phone upstairs. Mark began preparing Joe's meals, doing the dishes, and keeping the house clean. Both of them really enjoyed each other's company, and filled a need that neither really knew they had.

As time went on and familiarity set in, each became, how shall we say, more honest with each other. Soon, Joe found it much more convenient to just yell up the stairs from his chair whenever he needed Mark. But many times, Mark couldn't hear him because he had his own television on. And this didn't set very well with Joe.

So, Mark thought up the idea to give him a pizza pan and a soup ladle so he could hit it whenever he needed him. Mark thought his Grandpa would only need to hit it hard one time in order to get his attention. But that apparently wasn't the case as Mark explained, "Grandpa liked to hit on the pizza pan like it was a drum.... Bam-Bam-Bam-Bam!" And that obviously irritated Mark.

Mark was not without his share of faults either. His passion for watching professional wrestling, and getting a little loud while doing so, was well known throughout the Hublar Family. One day Joe's next-door neighbor asked Linda if she thought Mark might be abusive to his Grandpa. Linda was totally shocked by that question, and asked him why he would think such a thing. He responded, "I can occasionally hear Mark yelling at the top of his lungs."

But Linda laughingly explained the misunderstanding, saying, "With Mark's television being located upstairs, and the two houses being less than 10 feet apart, what the neighbor was actually hearing was an over enthusiastic wrestling fan, and not an abusive grandson. It appears that even the neighbors had some adjusting to do with this new arrangement!"

Mark always knew that it was ultimately his Grandpa's house, and that Joe would have the final say. And Mark always respected that. If either one of them ever had a serious complaint, they knew they could confide in Linda and that she would find a way to work it out.

Mark loved his companionship with his Grandpa, and the feeling of knowing that he was helping him to stay out of a nursing home. And Joe loved having Mark around. And he readily recognized the fact that because of Mark, he was able to stay in his own home.

Mark cooked breakfast for both of them every morning, and made a sandwich for his Grandpa's lunch every day. Linda prepared the evening meal ahead of time and would drop it off before she went to work each day. Then Mark would heat the meals so they could eat dinner together every night.

The two bachelors spent a lot of time together and enjoyed watching sports on television. Mark always made sure his Grandpa had a glass of ice water and the TV Guide on the end table next to his chair. And Mark concluded each night by helping his Grandpa get ready for bed, before he himself went upstairs to bed. Mark truly was Grandpa's angel on earth!

Life for these two continued on, and most days went very smoothly. The arrangement proved to be mutually beneficial, not to mention the fact that it brought Linda great peace of mind. But about the time life had settled into a nice routine, it would once again change for these two bachelors.

Mark's younger brother Greg, who was married to Lisa and now had two kids, Amber and Mason, were looking for a temporary place to stay while they were building a new home. Linda offered Grandpa's basement as a possible rent-free solution. To say this was an unfinished basement would be a bit of an understatement. This was the same basement that Linda would roller skate in as a child years before. But unafraid of a little hard work, and the motivation to save a few dollars for the new house, Greg and Lisa rolled up their sleeves, put on their protective gloves, masks, and glasses, and got to work.

They spent several days scraping mold off the cinder block walls, before washing them with bleach, and painting them a warm brown color that brought a sense of peace and tranquility. Next, they called in an exterminator to get rid of the pests that had taken up residency in the basement. This included camel crickets, which are the large brown bugs with long legs that actually come toward you as if they were preparing to defend their turf. Lastly, with Buddy's assistance, they properly hooked up their washer and dryer, and put curtains on all five of the small basement windows.

The basement even had a working toilet, and a shower that only needed the wraparound shower curtain to be replaced. They sectioned off the basement into an area for the beds, the television, a play area for the kids, and an office area for Greg. Truth be told, it was perfect. Not to mention it brought new life back to a previously ageing and decaying basement.

Speaking of new life, when Greg and his family moved in, it is safe to say the energy level in that house hit highs it hadn't experienced in decades. Linda, beaming with a gleam in her eyes, lovingly recalled the time, saying "When Greg, Lisa, Amber, Mason, and even their dog Abby moved in, it was like a breath of fresh air. Something about having a young family in that house made it come alive again!" It was the first time Joe had had a swing set in his back yard in over fifty years. And something he would love to laugh about when telling this to his card playing friends who would come over to play euchre.

To this day, Linda loves hearing the story of how Greg and Lisa were watching television in the living room when they continued to hear a motorized noise coming from the back of the house where his Grandpa would watch television in his lift assisted recliner. Greg went into detail, saying "We continued to hear the same noise that would last for about 5 seconds, pause momentarily, and continue for another five seconds. This went on for several minutes before I finally had to find out what was causing that noise. And much to my surprise, I saw Grandpa being lifted into a standing position by his chair, before being eased back in the same way to his previously sitting position. Mason had found the button on the chair and was giving Grandpa continuing lifts up and down in his chair." Greg concluded,

"Although I was horrified in the moment, Grandpa, grinning from ear to ear, could only say: "He's O.K., He's O.K.!"

Joe was happy to have two grandsons living in his house. He enjoyed the entertainment that his great grandchildren provided, and the blessing of having a family living with him again, even if it was on a temporary basis. No doubt, being the giver that Joe was, he had to feel blessed to again be able to provide for a part of his extended family in a very significant way. And Mark was thrilled, because he felt like his brother was "back home" with him again.

But soon it was time for Greg and his family to move into their new home, and life once again settled back into a calmer groove for the two bachelors. No more kids running up and down the stairs. No more compromises or adjustments that always come with the merging of families into the same living area. But, while the peace and quiet returned to the house, so too, did a bit of the emptiness.

Time continued to move on, and it had now been three years since Mark first moved in with his Grandpa. Joe was now in his early nineties, and mobility even with his walker, had become a challenge. Looking back on this time, the depth of Mark's love for his Grandpa may never fully be understood in this lifetime. But clues can be found in reflecting back on the level of devotion and commitment Mark displayed.

Each morning Mark would help his Grandpa to use the restroom, and to get him dressed in the morning. He continued making his meals and attending to his needs throughout the day. And would conclude each day, by again assisting him in the restroom before getting him into bed for the night. Linda continued to make the dinners, provide the bathing, do the grocery shopping, pay the bills, and provide transportation to dialysis, as well as to Sunday Masses. The efforts of Mark and Linda were obviously a huge blessing for Joe. It had kept Joe out of a nursing home, while providing him with some much-needed companionship.

Through those years, Joe was able to bond with Mark in a way he never could have imagined. How in the world this boy born with Down syndrome, who was told would never walk or talk, sit up or even be able to feed himself, and but for the faith of a young couple would have been sent to an unimaginable hell hole, where he no doubt would have laid in his own filth, hidden from the rest of the world, have been able to provide life extending services to a man in his nineties is something only God can answer.

But the bewilderment certainly wasn't lost on Joe. He confided in Linda, saying, "When Mark was born, I worried how you would ever be able to take care of him. Who would have ever imagined that he would grow up to take care of me?"

Soon, even Mark and Linda's most valiant efforts combined couldn't safely provide the care that Joe would require. Linda recalled the day that Joe knew it was time to move on, as he sadly told her, "Linda, I think it is time for Plan B." He added, "Just don't forget where I am."

Joe told Mark that he could have his bedroom. But Mark never did take him up on his offer. He wanted to keep it just the way his Grandpa had left it, just in case he came home for a visit. That day would never come as Joe died soon after entering the nursing home. Mark was devastated when he got the news. He loved his Grandpa with a love that most of us can't even comprehend. And now Mark was very lonely, and needed to find a way to fill the void.

But, as it was previously mentioned, when things aren't the way they should be, Mark goes to work on a solution. And the solution he came up with was in the joy and companionship that only man's best friend could provide. So, with his own money, he paid to have the back yard fenced in. And soon brought home a German Shepard puppy that he named Princess. This was not only a welcome distraction from the heartache Mark was feeling, but also turned out to be a key step in Mark's healing process!

Joe's spirit lives on in the lives that he touched. And his generosity extends beyond just the days he lived on this earth. As demonstrated in the fact that after Joe had passed and his will was read, it was discovered he left the option for Linda to be able to purchase her childhood home for a single dollar. His only stipulation was that Mark be allowed to live there as long as he wanted. Linda accepted the offer and "purchased" the house.

Mark eventually accepted his Grandpa's previous offer and moved his bed and furniture into what use to be Joe's bedroom. Once again, God had equipped the called by providing a home that Mark could call his very own! Mark continued to live in his new home for another thirteen years, returning to the bachelor life he had known three years earlier.

Chapter 9: My Time In The Workforce

Mark has always enjoyed his independence. And he has never asked for, nor ever expected, a free ride in order to maintain his independence. He grew up watching his father go to work every morning, sometimes coming home after he had already gone to bed.

As a business consultant most of his life, Mark's dad always had a home office in which Mark frequently saw him sitting behind his desk. Mark would try to emulate his father by grabbing a book and simply writing the words that were on no particular page onto a piece of paper. Although Mark didn't fully comprehend the words he was writing at the time, he unknowingly was developing a work ethic that would serve him well later in life.

At a young age Mark saw his older brother Mike working as a newspaper delivery boy for the New Albany Tribune. Later he saw his younger brother Greg working in the same capacity. Work, as with the overwhelming majority of us, is just part of making our way through this world. Mark understood this and looked forward to the day when he too would begin making his own money.

Mark has never been afraid of hard work. So, it wasn't long before he and Greg would walk the neighborhood streets after a good snowfall looking for driveways to shovel. Greg, never afraid to speak to other people, would be the front man and would negotiate the deal. He and Mark would shovel snow from the driveways and the sidewalks before walking back to the hopefully satisfied customer in order to collect their pay.

Mark was very strong and would always carry his fair share of the load. So, at the end of the day, the pay would always be evenly distributed between the two. This as much as anything began to instill into Mark, one of his most fundamental concepts that he preaches around the country today. And that is the concept of: "Equal Pay for Equal Work".

To this day, Buddy likes to recall a particular story of when these two young entrepreneurs learned their first lesson in upfront negotiations. It was early in their snow shoveling career, as they were eager to make some much-needed money. Money which would be spent on such things as posters, black lights, records, candy and other essentials at the time. Greg knocked on one particular neighbor's door, while Mark stood beside him with his shovel in hand ready to get to work. The elderly lady was very nice and accepted their offer to provide snow shoveling services.

She was familiar with these two kids, as they lived right down the street. The services were dutifully performed and were met with her approval. As she walked away from the door to retrieve their payment, visions of "big money" danced through the boy's heads. She quickly returned to proudly hand Greg four dollars to which he responded: "Do you have anything for my brother, he worked too!" She laughed and returned with two more dollars. From that moment forward, all fees were negotiated prior to the first snowflake being removed.

As a growing boy, Mark also took pride in cutting grass around the house. His childhood home sits on two acres of land, which was a little much for any of the boys at the time to cut by themself. Besides, each of the boys were looking for ways to make money. So, in order to keep the peace, the work had to be divided. In any case, Mark has always been capable of working, and has always expected to work, just like his brothers.

While Mark struggles with understanding exact dollar amounts, he fully understands the concept of working hard and making his own money. Mark has always been willing to work. However, his finding a legitimate opportunity to work, has never really been easy. And unfortunately, it remains a problem for many people like Mark all across the globe. This is a message that both Mark and Al would soon travel the country in order to promote, and to advocate for.

After graduating from New Albany High School in 1983, it was time for Mark to begin working full time. Sadly, unlike his brothers, college was not an option for someone with Down syndrome. His only option was to try and find a job. But in 1983, mainstream jobs weren't readily available for those with Down syndrome. Nor were they available for many others who had various types of handicaps.

Buddy and Linda have always been resolved to give Mark every possible opportunity to achieve his full potential, no different than their other three sons. And they certainly were not about to let him sit at home and live off the government for his survival. And besides, Mark genuinely wanted to work and would often tell his parents, "I don't want to sit at home and be a couch potato!" So, a solution had to be found.

Rauch Industries, located in New Albany, Indiana was one of the few programs at the time that even offered employment opportunities for those with disabilities. It was considered a sheltered workshop and afforded their employees the opportunity to perform somewhat repetitive tasks, mostly on a piecework basis. After some discussion between the three of them, and a review of the facility, it was decided that this is where Mark would begin his career.

Linda recalled the time, saying, "We all three thought the workshop would provide good training, and would be a good transition period for Mark." Al confirmed the thought, noting, "There is a big difference between attending classes and preparing to earn a living. We believed it would be a good way to prepare Mark for the future, as well as getting him the training that he needed to get a mainstream job in the community."

Mark initially enjoyed working at his new job. He was able to go to work like his dad, and now had the opportunity to make his own money. Rauch provided bus service to and from work which was a very nice benefit. In addition, Mark had several friends and acquaintances that were already employed at Rauch. It seemed like the perfect fit.

However, Mark was much more advanced than the average employee there. And he eventually became bored with many of the tasks he was assigned to do. These included jobs like sorting screws, filling salt packets, and working on a paint line. He especially hated it when they ran out of projects, and the workers filled the "down time" with coloring or watching a movie or TV. And to make matters worse, since the jobs were piece work in nature, the compensation was also based on the number of pieces completed. So, his paychecks would rise and fall with the level of work that was available during any given two-week period.

For Mark, if something isn't legitimate, he knows it. Not to say the workshop was not legitimate, because it provided, and continues to provide, employment for those in need. But Mark was capable of so much more, and he knew it. Mark, having a history of making money shoveling snow, cutting grass, and doing other odd jobs, was accustomed to making at least what he considered a fair amount. However, during slow times, Mark's check would not rise to the level of his expectations, and he wasn't shy about letting people know.

Buddy and Linda laughed as they recalled his supervisor telling them that he hated paydays because he knew Mark would be in his office to complain. In fairness to Mark, on one occasion, his two-week paycheck amounted to only twenty-six dollars. To say Mark wasn't happy about this would be a great understatement. And no doubt, this experience planted the seeds for the work Mark would do later in life, advocating on behalf of himself and his friends that people with disabilities need real work with real pay!

Mark continued to work at Rauch Industries for five years. It taught him several life lessons, and helped him prepare to enter the mainstream workforce. Buddy and Linda are very grateful for the opportunity that Rauch Industries provided to Mark. And over the years, they have supported the Rauch organization by attending events and informing others of the good works this organization continues to provide to those in need.

Mark's sister-in-law Lisa, spent twelve years as a Developmental Specialist with Rauch, Inc. Rauch is truly a blessing for many families in the area who have a family member with Down syndrome, or other types of mental challenge. For more information on the expanded services that Rauch Industries can now provide, please visit them on the web at www.rauchinc.org.

Mark's next big opportunity came when his father purchased an auto parts remanufacturing company in Louisville, Kentucky. D & W Sales was a remanufacturer of auto parts such as starters, alternators, brakes, clutches and water pumps. They distributed these products throughout the Midwest, as well as up and down the east coast. Al, with the backing of a local businessman turned investor, purchased the company and changed the name to Ace Remanufacture, Inc.

Soon after, he moved the company across the river and into New Albany, Indiana. The company began operating in two large buildings formerly occupied by Hoosier Panel. No one was more excited about this opportunity than Mark. He would now have a full-time job that paid him by the hour, and provided medical insurance, as it did to all of its one hundred plus employees.

This job was a dream come true for Mark. Working for his dad and seeing his brothers every day were perfect days for him.

Although Mike was married at the time and working in Kokomo, Indiana, it wouldn't be long before he returned to New Albany and joined his father.

Greg was still attending classes at Indiana University in Bloomington, but would come home and work during the summers. Upon graduation, Greg officially joined his father and brothers working at Ace. Mark's youngest brother Todd was still in high school, but also participated by making local deliveries to auto shops, and maintaining the grounds. Linda worked for three years as the company receptionist. And even Joe Stemle, Linda's dad, worked five days a week cleaning starter drives in the plant. This truly was a family atmosphere, and Mark couldn't have been happier.

Mark's primary role at Ace Remanufacture was more custodian in nature. He would use an industrial sweeper to keep the shop floors clean. And he collected trash from the various departments on a daily basis.

Both of these duties gave him the opportunity to speak with employees throughout the plant, as well as the warehouse. And as anyone who has ever spoken to Mark can attest, Mark has an innate ability to make people feel good about themselves, just by being himself. And many employees would actually look forward to seeing Mark making his rounds throughout the day!

As hard as Mark likes to work, I would dare say he likes to talk even more. These roles gave him the ability to do both. But his favorite job was operating the cardboard compactor. One day his dad came back from an out-of-town trip to find a desk, with an executive chair behind it, a fan, and two chairs across from the desk, professionally arranged next to the cardboard compactor he operated.

When Al asked Mark what was going on, he told his dad that it was his office. When Al probed a little deeper, asking him why he had the two chairs across from his desk, Mark said it was there in case someone wanted to stop by to talk to him. Mark has never gotten special treatment, and it wasn't about to begin on Al's watch. The next day the makeshift office was promptly disassembled!

Mark worked at Ace Remanufacture for five years before the company was sold. During this time, Mark had been working forty hours a week, earning a good salary with medical benefits.

The life lessons he learned, and the discipline he continued to develop, further prepared him for future employment. He did real work and received real pay.

This was very important to Mark as he was living on his own and paying his own bills. Independence, and the respect that came from making his own way, have always been driving forces in Mark's life. And if he wanted to continue living on his own, he would now have to find another way to generate the necessary income.

So, all on his own, and without informing his parents, he went into the McDonalds located on Charlestown Rd in New Albany, and asked to speak to the manager. Upon meeting with the manager, Mark informed him that he would like a job. Three days later, Mark was the newest member of the McDonald's organization.

In the beginning he wiped off tables and picked up papers in the parking lot. This gave Mark the opportunity to interact with customers, and he would always bring a smile to their face. Mark's consistent effort and good attitude eventually earned him the "Employee of the Month" Award! Soon after he was promoted to a cooking position in the kitchen!

Most of the employees were friendly, but occasionally there were some that were disrespectful toward him. But those occurrences were few, and usually involved a younger kid who more than likely didn't want to be working in the first place.

Mark enjoyed his time working at McDonalds and was employed for five years. However, when Mark's grandfather Joe, who was 90 years old at the time, began to experience mini strokes while still living on his own, Mark felt a higher calling. He quit his job, moved out of his one-bedroom home, and moved into his Grandfather's home in the hopes of keeping Joe out of a nursing home.

Taking care of Joe became Mark's new full time Job, and he loved it. He grew extremely close to his grandfather while enabling him to live at home for another three years. As previously mentioned, after his grandfather's passing, Mark stayed in that home for another thirteen years. But in order to do that, he was going to have to find another job.

Soon a job opportunity became available for Mark at Floyd County Memorial Hospital in New Albany. His main responsibility was washing silverware, as well as pots and pans. This job provided real work and real pay for Mark. It allowed him to continue to live on his own by earning enough money to cover all of his monthly expenses.

Like his time at Ace, on most days Mark rode his moped to and from work. However, unlike Ace, not everyone liked to speak with Mark. He worked with mostly women, some of whom were jealous that he was making as much money as they were. And some were very hostile toward him. There was no real social interaction and he ate all of his meals by himself.

Mark requested the opportunity to deliver meals to the patients, but was denied. No doubt he could have lifted the spirits of nearly every patient in that hospital! But the supervisors didn't believe he had the ability to deliver the right meals to the right rooms. However, they did allow him the opportunity to mix it up a bit by wrapping the silverware into a napkin and preparing the dinner trays.

Mark was a good worker and never missed a day. However, he did have one blemish on his record. It was made clear to all the workers that overtime was not allowed. And on one particular night, 8:00 pm rolled around a little quicker than expected, signifying the end of Mark's shift.

There were still a couple of pots and pans that needed to be cleaned. Mark made the decision to hide the remaining dirty pots and pans for the next day. This was a mistake that nearly got him fired. Other than that, Mark was no different than anyone else working to make a living and getting the job done!

Mark continued working at the hospital for five years. Unfortunately, Betty Morgan, the manager who gave Mark his opportunity, retired. And when the hospital brought in a consultant to review operations, Mark was informed that his position had been eliminated. While Mark was somewhat sad, he was also somewhat relieved that he wouldn't have to perform that particular job, in that particular environment any longer.

But reality wasn't lost on Mark. He ultimately knew what he had to do, if he wanted to maintain his independence and the bachelor lifestyle, he had become so accustomed to living. And that was to dust himself off and find a new job!

Mark's oldest brother Mike recommended he look into a job at Walmart. There was a relatively new location on Grant Line Road in New Albany, which could allow Mark to continue to ride his moped to and from work. So, Mike took Mark to Walmart to fill out an application, and to a subsequent interview with Terry Allen, the store manager.

Terry told Mike that he didn't need him to sit in the interview, as this meeting would only be between himself and Mark. Terry had a straight talk with Mark and clearly laid out his expectations before offering him a job stocking shelves in the Health and Beauty Department. Mark was thrilled at the opportunity to once again make his own money and have his own benefits, which included insurance.

Terry treated Mark like any other employee and expected him to do the work that he was assigned. Mark showed up every day, on time, and did the work he was asked to do. However, there was one problem. Mark couldn't seem to control his need to be social.

Al describes a time that after only three months, he got a call from Terry, saying, "He told me that Mark's employment was not going to work out. He said Mark is capable of doing the work, but he just can't stop talking." Terry had tried him in several different jobs that did not require him to interact with customers, but Mark just couldn't seem to stop talking.

In an attempt to lighten the mood, Al responded to Terry in a joking manner, saying, "Don't you have a job where Mark can get paid for just talking?" And much to Al's surprise, Terry said, "Yes." Turns out they had a position called customer greeter. Al concluded, "And the rest is history!" Mark worked for Walmart as a customer greeter for the next five and a half years.

Linda proudly chimed in, "That job was a match made in heaven for Mark. The employees were very nice and treated Mark with respect. And the best part was that he loved the customers and the customers loved him!" Al agreed, explaining, "This was a perfect fit for Mark as he was able to use his three biggest talents in developing his skills as a customer greeter – Confidence, Caring, and Organization!" Al continued by emphatically stating, "Mark was the best greeter Walmart ever had, or ever will have!"

Al backed up his bold statement by recounting the following story that occurred several years after Mark left Walmart, saying, "I was shopping at Walmart and a woman came up to me and asked me if I was Mark's father. She said that she really missed Mark and that she would always make sure her hair was fixed before going to Walmart because Mark would always tell her that she looked beautiful." Al concluded, saying "Who would expect a Walmart greeter to do that?"

Unfortunately, Mark began experiencing recurrent episodes of gout in his feet. Gout is a form of arthritis characterized by severe pain, redness, and tenderness in the joints. Pain and inflammation occur when too much uric acid crystallizes and deposits in the joints. It can be extremely painful and can make standing nearly impossible.

In addition, Mark was hospitalized twice for a blood clot in his leg. The doctor felt that standing for such long stretches throughout the workday may be contributing to these conditions. So, after five and a half years, Mark sadly resigned from Walmart.

Before he left, he was given a Five-Year Medal for exemplary performance. The event was even covered by a local TV station. You can view coverage of this event on the Photo/Video Gallery page of Mark's website at www.markjhublarspeaks.com.

After Mark left Walmart, he went to work for his dad. Together they started a company called Woodside Management where he worked full time. This company manufactured bed foundations, which is the part of the bed that supports the mattress.

Al reflected back on this time, "Our plan was to join forces with a local bed foundation manufacturer that had been struggling, and to grow that organization by hiring individuals with disabilities while paying them a real wage. It was a business that was in financial trouble, so the going was not easy. But we did manage to make it work, at least for a while."

Around the same time, this driven duo partnered with James Emmett, a well-known disability consultant, to form a consulting firm called "DisAbution." They received a substantial contract to travel the state of Ohio and talk to some large companies about hiring individuals with disabilities. Al would create specific power point presentations, and Mark would do the speaking.

Al had always known that many companies, even today, are still unaware of the potential that individuals with disabilities possess, and the loyalty and dedication they bring to an organization. This is a message that Al has dedicated a significant part of his life getting out to the business world and beyond.

Unfortunately, it wasn't long after they had things up and running with both companies that a near tragedy struck. After a five-mile run through the neighborhood, Al became dizzy to the point of not being able to keep his eyes open. Linda rushed him to the hospital where it was discovered he had suffered a heart attack.

Thankfully Al survived it, as well as the bypass and heart valve replacement that followed. However, this led to the closing of the consulting business, and the selling of Woodside Management to one of their largest customers.

As previously mentioned, Mark has always been very disciplined and organized. He has always laid his clothes out the night before work, set his alarm clock, and with very rare exception, gone to bed when he is supposed to. He wakes up with the alarm clock all on his own. And if he wakes up a little early, most times he will simply wait for the alarm clock to go off before his feet actually hit the floor. Mark has always been extremely consistent and has always maintained a good attitude.

But, in full disclosure, this consistency does come with a price. And that price is that Mark has one speed in which he operates, and one speed only. It is not a slow speed, but it doesn't increase when the heat is on. And any effort to increase that speed, or to get him out of his rhythm, is simply futile. That is why it has always been so important for Mark to find the type of work for which he is best suited. And no doubt, his God given talents and expertise can be found in how he interacts with other people.

The jobs that Mark has held over the years provided the revenue he needed to maintain his independence. But little did anyone know just how well these years had prepared Mark for what the Lord had planned for him, even from before his birth! That of being a Self-Advocate who would soon begin traveling the country on behalf of himself, his friends, and the countless others who continue to search for what Mark has termed R.O.I. – Respect, Opportunity, and Inclusion!

Mark continues to advocate on behalf of a whole class of people with untapped potential that are not only looking for an opportunity, but many who would end up being the most dedicated, loyal, and productive employees a company could ever hope to find. If only they were to be given a chance.

Chapter 10: A Time To Speak Up For Others

From the time Mark learned how to speak, it seemed like he was always advocating for someone. Whether it was running to tell his mother that his new born baby brother Greg was crying, to later sticking up for any of his brothers whenever they got into a scuffle with neighborhood friends, Mark has never held back from standing up for someone whom he thought needed help.

So, when Mark was offered the opportunity to speak to a group of kids at a local grade school on the topic of having Down syndrome, he was more than willing to accept. Being in his thirties, little did anyone know that this would be the start of something that would grow into a career for Mark. And more importantly, it would be the start of a movement that continues to fulfill the Lord's will in the lives of an untold number of people, who need Mark to speak out on their behalf.

It was at this time when Richard Williams, a previous neighbor, asked him to be a guest speaker at his daughter's school. It was Disability Week at Our Lady of Perpetual Help Parochial School.

This is the same school that Mark's three brothers attended. And the parish in which his entire family still attends to this day.

Richard asked Mark to talk to a class about what it was like to have Down syndrome. Mark was more than happy to oblige. He even brought his photo album along to pass around to show special events in his life, and things that he had accomplished. This included various pictures of the time he had been a Cub Scout, and even the time he played on the school's football team with his brother Greg.

Even then Mark was trying to impress upon the boys and girls that people with disabilities are "More alike than different." And for a special effect, Mark kicked the side of an empty desk and said to the class, "This hurts my foot just like it would hurt your foot." Mark has always had an uncanny ability to make the biggest statements with the smallest of words!

Mark was a natural. And Linda and Buddy who attended the event for support, were absolutely blown away. They had always known that Mark was passionate. And that he has the purest of hearts. But they had no way of knowing exactly how that passion and purity would translate to his audience in terms of being able to communicate the message he wanted to deliver: That of him being "More Alike Than Different" from themselves.

The fears that no doubt churned in the pit of Buddy and Linda's stomach moments before Mark began his talk, soon turned to relief. And then into overwhelming joy and amazement! Buddy took a more philosophical approach in remembering that momentous occasion, saying, "Mark did a great job following his note cards. And that helped him to stay on point."

However, there would soon be no doubt that in that very moment, in front of a group of grade school students, a calling for Mark's life had been revealed. And his parents were there to witness it all! Soon, the never ceasing wheels that continually spin in Al's brain, were picking up speed again. The Lord had opened his heart a little wider, revealing his plan for the next phase of Mark's life.

When asked about how Mark became a public speaker, Al reflected back to the beginning of Mark's career, saying, "When Mark first started giving talks, his mother and I thought it would just be for fun. However, when we saw how serious Mark was about his message, we realized that he definitely had something to say, and that his message could resonate with individuals, parents, businesses, government organizations, as well as groups that were interested in helping individuals with disabilities live a full life!"

Linda recalled the start of Mark's professional public speaking career in a similar way, saying, "Buddy got the idea for Mark to speak publicly. He believed Mark now had an important message to tell other parents. One that would give hope, and inspire them to believe that their children could have a bright future, as well as live an independent life."

Linda also pointed out the fact that, "Demonstrated by his many stage performances of Elvis and Michael Jackson, Mark no doubt is a born entertainer!" She concluded her thoughts on the matter, saying, "And Al thought by combining Mark's love of the stage with his ability to speak out for others, that it just might be possible for him to earn a living, and actually have a career doing what he loves, just like his brothers."

At a Down syndrome conference in Kansas City, Buddy and Linda watched a workshop presentation given by a young man with Down syndrome. At that time, it was most unusual to have a room full of people listening to someone speaking with Down syndrome. They noticed this young man's brother was operating a slide projector that would project a picture onto the screen. And while each individual picture was being projected, this special speaker would talk about a story that gave life to that picture, and the circumstances that surrounded the story. And after finishing with one photo, he would motion for his brother to go to the next photo until the message he was delivering to his audience was complete.

Linda vividly recalled the event, noting, "Something must have clicked in Al's brain, because that is when the idea of Mark using a power point for his presentations was born." Al knew that if Mark was going to get serious about being a professional public and motivational speaker, then he would have to take a critical, but objective, view of the challenges that Mark would face in delivering his message.

Al shared his findings, saying: "Mark is a natural speaker, but he has always had trouble staying on topic, and understanding the importance of sticking to a defined time limit. In addition, it can be difficult for a large audience to understand everything that

Mark says." Al was referring to Mark's somewhat raspy voice, and how he has problems with words either starting with the letter "R", or ones that have a long "R" sound in them.

Relying on his years as a business consultant, Al knew he had successfully identified the key obstacles to Mark's success. Now all he had to do was find an effective solution to each of those obstacles.

As Al reflected back on what he saw in Kansas City, he quickly determined that using a PowerPoint presentation had the potential to remove all three of the above obstacles. He explained, "By uploading pictures into the presentation, and listing the major points beside each picture, Mark would not only be able to clearly and concisely get his message across, but would also be able to stay on point, and thus on time."

Al continued, "This combination of having bullet point notes, listed next to a specific picture that was being projected on a screen for the whole audience to see, enables those who otherwise might have a challenge understanding Mark to easily follow along and not miss an important point."

Al proudly concluded, "However, the real key to Mark's successful speaking engagements is how he so naturally speaks from his heart. His sincerity allows him to connect with his audience, almost on a spiritual level, by putting into his own words, his individual thoughts and feelings of what each topic or event means to him!"

Soon doors would begin to open and opportunities for Mark to spread his message became more frequent. Mark's passion for advocating for those with disabilities would soon reach heights that no one could have ever imagined. His message of "Respect, Opportunity, and Inclusion," and of being "More Alike Than Different," went from the venues of local elementary and high schools, to speaking at nationally known colleges such as Indiana University, University of Kentucky, and Pennsylvania State University. And he has addressed audiences from world-wide companies such as Wal-Mart.

In May of 2019, Mark gave an inspiring speech at the Volunteers of America (VOA) Midstate's Fourth Annual *Building Better Communities* Luncheon which raised funds for their programs in Clark and Floyd Counties in Indiana.

Volunteers of America continues to play an important role in Mark's success as he takes advantage of the many services they offer. These include providing him transportation to the grocery store, shopping for clothes, and even taking him to social events. VOA not only helps Mark find speaking engagements, but also helps him prepare various Power Point presentations. In short, they are instrumental in Mark's efforts to achieve a full and meaningful life.

Volunteers of America is a faith-based nonprofit organization founded in 1896 that provides affordable housing and other assistance services primarily to low-income people, including veterans, low-income seniors, children and families, the homeless, those with disabilities, recovering addicts and the formerly incarcerated. More information on this important organization can be found at www.voa.org.

Mark has traveled to our nation's capital to personally advocate to members of the United States Congress. He has spread his message of hope and inspiration across the country from Connecticut to Washington State. And even traveled down to Austin Texas, where he was the keynote speaker at a conference of teachers from all across the state of Texas. Highlights of this particular speech can be seen by visiting the Photo/Video Gallery page on Marks website at www.markjhublarspeaks.com.

This life affirming integrity, which flows openly and honestly from Mark's heart to those he is speaking to, is really what moves his audiences. His ability to personalize a story just by seeing a picture or recalling an event, translates into an honesty and a credibility that few speakers anywhere possess. It is a sincerity that has moved his audiences from the lowest of lows to the highest of highs, all in the same speech. From actual tears that well up in the eyes of his listeners, to the biggest of smiles leading to outright joyful laughter.

Mark unapologetically takes his audience through a range of emotions by unabashedly recalling the challenges and successes of his life. And he provides no nonsense, practical advice to those who are struggling to find a way forward in raising their own special needs child.

Following a presentation, parents of Down syndrome children love to meet Mark. They love hearing him speak, and want to learn more. And they generally tend to ask him two types of questions. One typically has to do with how he became such a successful speaker. And the other is in regards to any advice that he could give in terms of raising their special needs child.

Mark's response to the first question is typically brushed off with a nod being given to his brothers. But the second type of question evokes a more heartfelt and consistent answer. In its various forms, Mark's response to this type of question always includes the following takeaways: "Take them home and love them like you do your other children. Always treat them with respect. Give them the same opportunities you give your other children. And always include them in your family in everything you do!"

Mark's positive perspective and "can-do" attitude is very infectious. He is very encouraging to all those around him, and is constantly reminding others of how special they are in their own right. He is very generous with his complements and you can't help but feel good about yourself in his presence.

Mark's older brother Mike puts it into perspective this way, sharing, "Mark is definitely a special individual that once you meet him, you will never forget him. His impact on the Down syndrome community, and the community at large, is undeniable.

He has a way of challenging and humbling those of us close to him every time we are in his presence."

Mike continued, "Mark's positive and loving outlook also helps those that are lucky enough to encounter him, as they tend to take away a sense of confidence knowing that we are all good inside. It's a gentle reminder that we sometimes just need to step back from ourselves and breathe in the beauty around us."

Mark continues to speak across the county to businesses, educational institutions, government agencies, parent groups, and self-advocates about the importance of giving everyone ROI, which stands for Respect, Opportunities, and Inclusion.

Mark participates in government-sponsored programs to help individuals move out of nursing homes and workshops, and even start their own business. He currently represents the Work To Include / Employment First Initiative in Southern Indiana. Mark is also a member of a consulting group that is working with the Gallup Organization on a program to identify the talents and strengths of individuals with Down syndrome.

However, this list doesn't even begin to scratch the surface of what he has accomplished. Nor does it begin to explain the impact he has had on the countless lives who have heard him speak. If you would like more information on how you may be able to schedule Mark to speak at your event, please go to www.markjhublarspeaks.com.

Chapter 11: The People I Have Met

In Mark's pursuit of spreading his message of Respect, Opportunity and Inclusion, he has gotten the opportunity to travel the country. And in those travels Mark has met so many people from so many different walks of life. From struggling parents just looking for some hope and reassurance that their child will have a life worth living, to household names in which most anyone would be familiar.

His call to spread love and encouragement through simply sharing the experiences of his own life, has led him to cross paths with a variety of people. From professional athletes and coaches, to live entertainers and performers, to local and national politicians, to others whose own accomplishments have inspired people from across the country, and even around the world. Mark has not only had the opportunity to interact with some of these people, but no doubt, has also left his own impression on them.

One special characteristic that Mark possesses, can be found in the way he treats all people the same. He doesn't see the world as most people see it. He doesn't have any preconceived notions of what it means to be a celebrity of sorts. He only sees the good inside people. This is not to say that he doesn't have hero's, particularly members, both past and present, of his beloved Dallas Cowboys. As well as some country singers that he has shared the stage with.

But, in his entire life, Mark has never wished he were someone else. Not even for a minute. While at times, no doubt, he has longed to be able to do some of the things that others have been able to do, especially some of the things his brothers have been able to do, he has never once wished, or even questioned, why he was the one to be born with Down syndrome. He has always been more than comfortable in his own skin.

Simply put, Mark has just always known that each person is special in their own way. It is for the same reason Mark has trouble determining someone's age, that he doesn't get wrapped up in someone's stature or status. He only sees what's on the inside of the person in which he is speaking to. He fully believes that we are all children of our loving God. And that we are all special!

Mark's greatest gift to the world is how he makes everyone that he meets feel like a celebrity, no matter who you are, or what your story may entail. As his older brother Mike likes to say, "After speaking with Mark, a person simply cannot walk away from that conversation not feeling better about themselves!"

With all this said, it is still pretty cool when you learn of all the unique people that have crossed Mark's path throughout his journey. And thus, the decision to include this chapter was made.

Mark's advocacy on behalf of those with special needs has led him through the political arena. This includes meeting with politicians on the local, state, and even federal levels of government. His interactions have been both purposeful and memorable.

Like the time he met Patrick Kennedy, founder of the Congressional Down Syndrome Caucus, and son of the late Ted Kennedy. At that time, Patrick was a member of the House of Representatives. Mark traveled to Washington DC to meet with him, as well as other members of congress, to discuss a "Bill of Rights" for people born with disabilities.

When being introduced to the committee, Mark's last name was mispronounced using a short sounding "u", such as used in the word "Hub Cap". Mark has always been proud of his family. And as the members of congress quickly found out, he is also proud of the correct pronunciation of his family's name. As Mark immediately shouted out, "It's pronounced "Hublar" ("Who-blar"). This drew immediate chuckles from the members of congress. But it also set the tone that Mark was serious about the work he was there to accomplish!

Mark has also met with Todd Young, who is currently serving as the Senior United States Senator from Indiana, and who from 2011 to 2017 was the U.S. Representative for Indiana's 9th congressional district. Mark met with Senator Young to advocate for the passing of the ABLE Act. A.B.L.E. stands for Achieving a Better Life Experience. And the resulting ABLE accounts are tax-advantaged savings and investment accounts for individuals with disabilities.

According to the ABLE National Resource Center, "This effort originated with a group of parents of children with disabilities who recognized the unfairness of not being able to save funds in their child's name for fear of losing essential benefits, benefits that allow their child to live independently in the community." And as Mark does with everyone, he left a lasting impression on Senator Young.

Al will also never forget this particular meeting as he proudly recalled Mark strongly advocating for those with special needs. Mark, no stranger to finding a way to achieve whatever it is that he has set his sights on, spoke in a language he thought would resonate with his audience of one. And soon Mark got down to brass tacks with the senator.

Al explained the meeting this way, "After about an hour of discussion, Mark looked into Senator Young's eyes and said, "Todd, if you support us, we will support you!" Laughing with pride, Al went on to say, "Senator Young looked back at Mark and said, "Mark, you are without a doubt the most confident individual I have ever met – with or without a disability." What a ringing endorsement, and true description, of this incredible advocate for those with disabilities.

As many people may know, Sarah Palin is the former governor of Alaska, and a 2008 Vice Presidential Candidate. But what you may not know is that Sarah is also the mother of a child born with Down syndrome. Mark attended a breakfast in Sarah's honor hosted by a Down syndrome support organization called "S.M.I.L.E. on Down syndrome." Their Vision is "That all people with Down syndrome will be loved, respected, and accepted as valuable members of families and communities." The Acronym S.M.I.L.E stands for Support, Management, Information, Love, and Encouragement. Information on this organization can be found at www.smileondownsyndrome.org.

This organization is located in Evansville, Indiana, which just happens to be the same city where Mark's younger brother, Todd, was playing college football at the time for the Evansville Purple Aces. So, Mark was excited to be able to see Todd again, and also be able to meet Sarah Palin all in the same trip. Mark's encounter with Sarah was another opportunity for him to encourage yet another mother who happened to have a young child with Down syndrome. And as is typical, Mark didn't disappoint.

When Sarah asked Mark if he had any advice regarding her own son with Down syndrome, Mark simply looked deep into her eyes and told her, "Just love him and include him in everything." Sometimes, it seems the fewer the words, the better the advice.

Mark is the master of making others feel good about themselves and is always going the extra mile to do so. In this case, Mark even purchased and presented Sarah with an Indiana Hoosier outfit for her special son to wear as a reminder of her trip to Indiana.

Mark's involvement with the many special organizations that have called upon his services has led him to meet, and even pose for pictures, with many people from across the professional sports world. This includes Pat Day, a well-known Horse Jockey who is a four-time winner of the Eclipse Award for Outstanding Jockey. Pat won nine Triple Crown races, as well as twelve Breeders' Cup races before retiring in 2005. Mark also very much enjoyed meeting and getting a picture taken with Evander Holyfield, a former World Heavyweight Boxing Champion, who attended the 2019 Gallop Gala in Louisville, Kentucky.

On a trip to Indianapolis for the D.A.D.S. convention, Mark was introduced to Tony Dungy. D.A.D.S. stands for Dads Appreciating Down Syndrome, and whose stated mission is: "To assist and support, through fellowship and action, the fathers and families of individuals with Down syndrome." This group prides themselves on being out in the community coaching their kids' sports teams, participating in their children's Individual Education Programs, volunteering at local Down syndrome fund-raising events, and even sponsoring fund-raising events of their own. You can learn more about this special organization by going to www.dadsnational.org.

Tony Dungy is known by many as a National Football League Analyst who won Super Bowl XII as a player with the Pittsburgh Steelers, as well as winning Super Bowl XLI as the head coach of the Indianapolis Colts. Mark was able to speak with Tony, as well as have his picture taken with him. Later the group went out on the field and practiced throwing and catching the football. Tony then signed a football for Mark, which he proudly displays in his apartment.

Mark has also met Karen Gaffney, the first person with Down syndrome to complete a relay swim of the English Channel in 2001. According to Wikipedia, her 2007 swim across the nine-mile span of Lake Tahoe became the subject of the documentary Crossing Tahoe: A Swimmer's Dream. And in 2009, she swam across Boston Harbor, a distance of five miles, to celebrate Down Syndrome Month in Massachusetts. She has also completed 16 swims across the San Francisco Bay on her way to receiving the

Global Down syndrome Quincy Jones Exceptional Advocacy Award in 2010.

One athlete Mark has met, who has remained near to his heart and for good reason, is Steve Green. Steve is a local basketball star hailing from Silver Creek High School in nearby Sellersburg, Indiana. Steve was Bobby Knight's first recruit to Indiana University in 1971, where he became a standout player for the Hoosiers. He went on to play for the Utah Stars of the American Basketball Association before playing for the Indianapolis Pacers of the National Basketball Association.

But for Mark, this paled in comparison to what he believed Steve's greatest accomplishment to be, that of being the father to a very special daughter, Jessica, who happened to be born with Down syndrome. Mark had originally met Jessica at a wedding reception. He subsequently met up with her again at a Capabilities Talent Show, where Jessica sang on stage, and where the two became good friends. With Steve's approval, the next year Mark took Jessica to the Down syndrome Joy Prom.

Linda fondly reflected back, saying: "I think Mark made Steve's day when he stopped as he was walking out the door, turned and shook Steve's hand, and thanked him for having such a beautiful daughter." That's just Mark's way. And to know him is to truly love him!

Mark has also met and befriended many entertainers and musicians. One of his favorites is Mark Maxwell, the lead singer of the band "The Louisville Crashers." Mark first saw this band at his niece's wedding reception. He became an instant fan and soon went to all of their concerts which included local venues such as the River Stage in Jeffersonville, Indiana and the Amphitheater in New Albany, Indiana.

Mark Maxwell has invited Mark to join him on stage many times, an impromptu invitation that Mark always accepts. He has even written a song for a Down syndrome talent show. But the nicest thing this very popular singer has ever done for Mark was not done in front of a large crowd, but rather far from public view. And that was surprising Mark by attending his graduation ceremony at Jefferson Community Technical College. Mark was blown away by this kind and sincere act, and so was his family.

Mark has also shared the stage with some country singers as well. Tayla Lynn, granddaughter of country singing legend

Loretta Lynn, is another one of Mark's musical friends. Mark first heard Tayla singing at the Corydon Jamboree in Corydon, Indiana and became an instant fan. Later He met her in person at a concert that was held at Loretta Lynn's Ranch, in Hurricane Mills, Tennessee. It was here that he officially joined her fan club.

Subsequently, Tayla learned of Mark's story and personally invited him to join her on stage at her next Indiana concert, in Mitchell, Indiana. It was here that Mark actually joined Tayla on stage and sang "Coal Miner's Daughter" together. Mark worked for weeks to memorize all the words to the song. And no doubt it was an experience that neither Tayla, nor Mark, will soon forget.

Mark has met so many people from so many different walks of life, it would be nearly impossible to share each of his experiences. However, he has met some special actors that bear mentioning. Chris Burke, who played the role of "Corky" on the television series "Life Goes On", is one such person.

Chris was born with Down syndrome and is also an Advocate. Like Mark, he too was born at a time when little was known about Down syndrome. According to Wikipedia, his parents were told to institutionalize Chris when he was born. Instead, they decided to raise him at home and nurture his talents, with the help of his two older sisters and brother.

The article went on to say that from a young age, Chris enjoyed watching TV and movies and wanted to be on television. He was encouraged by his supportive family to follow his career objectives no matter how unconventional they seemed, especially for a young man with Down syndrome.

Mark met Chris in Indianapolis at a Down syndrome Buddy Walk. The two later met again at a Capabilities Walk in New Albany, and afterward they spent some quality time together.

Another special person that Mark has had the privilege of meeting is David DeSanctis. David played the part of "Produce" in the movie, "Where Hope Grows." This is one of those rare movies that actually stars a person with Down syndrome, and that was released into movie theaters. In addition to being an accomplished movie actor, David is a Down syndrome Self-Advocate and Motivational Speaker.

Mark and David met through Down Syndrome of Louisville, where they presented a speech together for the Arc of Kentucky at the Crowne Plaza, in Louisville, Kentucky.

As was mentioned in the beginning of this chapter, Mark doesn't have any preconceived notions of what it means for someone to be a celebrity of sorts. He only sees the good inside people. He loves everyone that he meets and sincerely believes, in fact he knows, that everyone is special in their own right, and certainly in the eyes of God!

This is most evident in the fact that Mark can't even fathom the respect, love, and admiration that nearly everyone that he has ever met, has for him. Mark is humble beyond belief, and is no doubt a "celebrity" in his own right.

Chapter 12: My Greatest Accomplishments So Far

It would be fair to say that Mark's entire life has been a series of never-ending accomplishments. From the moment he was born, he escaped the fate of living a life trapped in an institution. He soon exceeded the developmental phases of a toddler, those in which his own doctor said he would never achieve. And he started attending school at the age of two.

Mark has made friends and played organized sports. He graduated from a mainstream High School. And incredibly graduated from College. He has worked real jobs for real money.

Mark lives independently and maintains his own residence. He has made a career of speaking out and advocating on behalf of others who cannot do so for themselves. And he influences the passing of laws that help protect those he speaks for. Mark's accomplishments have known no bounds!

Looking back to the beginning, Linda recalled the excitement of some of Mark's more memorable accomplishments as a newborn. After briefly allowing herself to feel some of the distant sadness from hearing the dim future and the negative impact Mark was projected to have on her family, she joyfully reflected back to how the doctors were so wrong when he told her all the things Mark would never be able to do. And the exhilaration she and Buddy felt as Mark continually proved the medical field wrong with each new accomplishment.

First Mark began sitting up on his own. Later he learned how to roll over, walk, talk, and eat from a spoon. All the while displaying a whole range of emotions! These were the first of Mark's accomplishments. And while these unimaginable and unpredictable milestones were celebrated in a fashion most parents could not even imagine, more importantly these accomplishments also allowed both Buddy's and Linda's optimistic imagination to run wild with questions of what else Mark may be able to accomplish. Little did they know at the time, they hadn't seen anything yet!

Mark learned how to ride a bike the same way his brothers did. It started with training wheels. And then with Buddy holding on to the bike while running along the side of him. And then finally on his own. But to say there weren't the typical scrapes, bruises, and occasional tears along the way, would only serve to cheapen his accomplishment.

From there he went on to learn how to ride a moped. And although his first experience was one that will never be forgotten, as it landed him unconscious in the middle of the road before being loaded into the back of an ambulance, both Mark and his parents remained undaunted. Mark, never one to walk away from a challenge, soon continued working on the finer points of mastering the art of riding a moped. And from there It wasn't long before he bought his own.

For years Mark owned a moped and frequently would ride it to Church, Kroger, the library, and other places around town. It has been a part of his independence and has represented his ability to overcome challenges.

Mark even earned his drivers permit and drove Linda around town for several months. However, missing just two more questions than allowed on the written portion of the driver's test, Mark decided a moped would suffice for his transportation needs. But nonetheless, what an accomplishment!

Mark's accomplishments in the classroom have also been another unexpected blessing. He loved school and was in fact upset at the very possibility of even having a snow day, or any other disruptions to his school schedule. This was one trait that he definitely did not share with any of his brothers.

Mark attended and graduated from special education classes at New Albany High School in 1983. But even this accomplishment was eventually surpassed by his actual going to college and graduating with a three-year degree from Jefferson Community & Technical College in Louisville, Kentucky in 2016. An accomplishment that required him to regularly take city buses by himself from one side of the Ohio River across to the other in order to attend classes.

A goal of obtaining a college degree originally was never even considered, let alone thought possible. But leave it to Mark to find a way to accomplish the impossible!

The opportunity for Mark to earn his college degree in Public Speaking was made possible in part with a scholarship awarded to him from Ruby's Rainbow. This organization was co-founded by Liz Plachta, after she and her husband brought home their beautiful daughter Ruby, who was also born with Down syndrome. Ruby's Rainbow is located in Austin, Texas and provides multiple college scholarships across the country each year to very deserving students with Down syndrome.

Ruby's Rainbow is funded by donations, as well as by sponsors, and relies heavily on the goodness of people from around the country who take their annual "3/21 Pledge." For more information on how you can contribute to this vital program, please visit www.rubysrainbow.org.

The National Down Syndrome Society is the leading human rights organization for all individuals with Down syndrome. They envision a world in which all people with Down syndrome have the opportunity to enhance their quality of life, realize their life aspirations, and become valued members of welcoming communities. They also contributed to Mark's success by making a donation which offset some of the expenses of going to college. More information on this very important organization can be found by visiting www.ndss.org.

In 2019, Mark was honored by Our Lady of Providence High School with their Community Service Award for outstanding work in the community. At the ceremony, the faculty surprised Mark by awarding him an honorary degree. Now Mark can officially say that he too graduated from Providence, just like his three brothers!

In addition to being a life-long supporter of Providence High School, Mark will always be a huge fan of their Hall of Fame Football Coach Gene Sartini, who happened to coach all three of his brothers. Mark is beloved by the Sartini family, who invited him to proceed with them during Gene's funeral procession down the High School Football Field that bears his name.

Gene made no secret that he too was a big fan of Mark's. A few years earlier, Gene surprised Mark by giving him an official Providence football jersey with Mark's last name added to the back. Today that same jersey hangs in a frame above Mark's television in his family room.

Some of Mark's greatest accomplishments have no doubt been the profound impact he has had advocating for others. Mark is a member of a consulting group that is working with the Gallup Organization on a program to identify the talents and strengths of individuals with Down syndrome. And he has appeared in a televised campaign created by the National Down Syndrome Congress reminding the country that people with Down syndrome are "More Alike Than Different!"

Mark has also appeared on local billboards as a part of his advocacy supporting the Work To Include initiative in Southern Indiana, which promotes Employment for Hoosiers with Disabilities. In addition, Mark has even been successful in his advocacy to pass important laws by meeting directly with lawmakers on Capitol Hill.

Mark has earned many awards and has been recognized and honored by numerous organizations for his accomplishments including, but not limited to, Down Syndrome of Louisville, Down Syndrome of Indiana, National Down Syndrome Congress, National Down Syndrome Society, The Wendy M. Wood Award - Indiana APSE, The Laura Lee Self-Advocate Leadership Award - Helen A. Keller Institute for Human Disability, The Face of Compassion Award - Center for Interfaith Relations, Ruby's Rainbow Scholarship and Ambassador Award, and the Indiana Institute on Disability and Community - Indiana University.

No matter how many accomplishments and awards Mark has racked up over his lifetime, the one quality that has remained constant throughout Mark's entire life is the unfathomable depth of his love for his family. From spending every waking moment learning from his older brother Mike, to the days when both of his younger brothers came home from the hospital for the first time, Mark's love and devotion to his brothers is legendary.

From running to get bottles and diapers anytime he heard his younger brothers cry, to teaching them everything he himself had learned, Mark has more than accomplished the role of being a brother that anyone would love to have. To this day, there is not a single thing that any of his brothers can think of that Mark would not do for them at the asking. His love and devotion have never once waivered or diminished in the slightest. But one of his biggest unforeseeable impacts is how he has unwittingly inspired his brothers to become better people.

Mike, who was there from the very beginning of Mark's life, has been a witness to all of Mark's accomplishments. When asked about his perspective, Mike responded, "Mark's greatest accomplishment is his development of a personal sense of joy and a seemingly never-ending positive attitude. I often refer to a quote from an unknown author who stated: "Life is comprised of 10% of what happens to you and 90% of how you react to it." And Mark is a daily reminder of just how inspirational this quote can be for me."

Mike went on to say, "Mark's positive attitude can motivate even the most stubborn realists to stop making excuses for themselves and take charge of their own destiny. Every time I am around Mark, I can't help but to feel that anything is possible if I would simply get out of my own way and allow myself to see the world through his eyes, even if just for a little while."

Mike wrapped up his perspective saying, "Mark's infectious joy and can-do attitude is truly making a difference in the world that he was born into. And it represents what it means to live a purposeful life regardless or your personal circumstances!"

Mike's wife Debra has also been a part of Mark's journey since way back in his high school days. And she shared her unique insights into Mark's many accomplishments, saying, "It's wonderful that Mark has been able to touch so many lives. It's a great accomplishment that just the story of Mark's life inspires and gives hope to the mothers and fathers of Down syndrome children everywhere. But to me, Mark's greatest accomplishment is just being the man he is."

She went on to explain, "When I've had the opportunity, over the forty some years I've known Mark, to have a one-on-one conversation with him, I'm reminded that he's just a person. A person that dreams, that loves, that gets lonely, that enjoys his hobby's, and that gets bored. He's a person that isn't afraid to be vulnerable, isn't afraid to try, isn't afraid to fail. He's a person that doesn't let life's disappointments get him down for long. He enjoys the simplest things in life."

Debra concluded by saying, "In my opinion, Mark's independence is his number one accomplishment. This includes his ability to live on his own, to keep his apartment neat and clean, to make his own meals, and to have a daily routine that promotes his health. A lot of folks that don't have Down syndrome, don't accomplish that!"

Linda, never one to miss an opportunity to heap praise on any of her four son's achievements, view's Mark's accomplishments as a Win / Win with his Brothers. She clarifies by saying, "Mark drew his brothers closer together, with all of them wanting to make life better for him!" Both Linda and Buddy love to see the closeness of their four sons that continues to this day. And it continues to warm their hearts to see Mark's brothers still inviting him to a variety of different events.

Some of these events are done on an individual basis, while others are done as a group. For example, Mark enjoys events such as going to rock concerts with Mike, cookouts on the deck and watching his beloved Dallas Cowboys with Greg, and attending live professional wrestling matches with Todd. Truth be told, Mark would go anywhere, for any reason, just to spend time with his brothers.

Mark's accomplishments are second to none. Especially in the face of the impossible odds he faced right from the start. The outright predictions of gloom and doom of those in the medical profession, including one doctor who told his parents that Mark would not even live to see his 20th Birthday.

But Mark's greatest accomplishment is one that not only is interwoven into each of his other accomplishments, but is also the single most important in anyone's life. And that is the fulfilling of the two greatest commands given by his Lord and

Savior, Jesus Christ: "To love God with all his heart, all his mind, and all his soul. And to love his neighbor as himself."

Mark has truly demonstrated what the fulfillment of these commands looks like. Mark does not have a mean bone in his body. And the love that people feel after encountering Mark is a direct result of the Lord's love flowing through him to the world.

No doubt the Lord had, and has, a plan for Mark's life. And there is also no doubt that up to this point, Mark has accomplished that plan. The only question left is, how many more achievements does the Lord have waiting for Mark to Accomplish?

Chapter 13: My Hopes And Aspirations

Mark's hopes and aspirations started out just like anybody else's. That being to understand his environment and to learn how to navigate throughout this life. Beginning with the natural ability to cry as a baby when he instinctively knew that he needed something. Such as the need to be fed, have his diaper changed, or simply the need to be held. Mark was born with the same needs as everyone else starting out in life.

Likewise, Mark continued to desire the same things most any other human child would want. The desire to begin manipulating his environment to accomplish and satisfy the desires he had. To be able to move independently by way of rolling over, crawling, setting up on his own, and to eventually being able to walk. To reach for things. To be able to hold things in his hand. And then like most toddlers, to ultimately put them into his mouth. To hold his own bottle and find various ways to soothe and entertain himself.

In these early phases of life, Mark was certainly more alike than different. It was only in the struggle to accomplish these most basic tasks, that his life would begin to take a unique path different from most of us.

However, like most of us, certain expectations were placed upon Mark from the beginning. With Buddy and Linda's steadfast commitment to treat him no different than they would any of his siblings, certain aspirations were required of him.

Mark would be taught to obey the same rules that his brothers would be required to follow. He would be held to the same standard of reaching his full potential, regardless of what level that might turn out to be. He would be required to carry his share of the load, regardless of the situation. And his brothers were there to make sure he didn't get any special treatment, or any favoritism along the way.

Al humbly recalled it this way, saying: "When we took Mark home from the hospital, we had no idea what to expect, or how we should raise him. We knew that we loved him and that we were willing to do whatever it took to give him a good life." He went on to say, "His three brothers had an innate feeling that he needed to be protected, but not spoiled. They did an excellent job of following that plan. They expected Mark to follow the same rules that they had to follow, and every day they taught him something new."

Little did any of Mark's brothers know at the time, they were actually helping him to understand personal responsibility, along with a sense of what is right and what is wrong. Greg gave his perspective by candidly sharing the following, "At the time, I didn't have a clue how this was impacting Mark. I just knew I didn't want to do any more work than I had to, and that Mark had to carry his own load!"

In hindsight, that attitude was allowed to be fostered as a result of Buddy and Linda's not crippling Mark by lowering the bar for him. His brothers only reflected and enforced the rules, both those explicitly stated and those implicitly learned, that were handed down from their parents. Thus, setting the foundation for Mark's understanding of fairness and the need to make sure others were also given the same opportunities to participate in whatever it was they were trying to do.

It wasn't long before Mark found his voice and began speaking up for others. It started, as most things typically do, at home amongst his family. Whether it would be standing up for himself, or feeling the need to back one of his brother's in a disagreement with a neighborhood friend, Mark's sense of justice was both undeniable, and soon, unstoppable.

As Mark continued growing older, so did his urge to speak his mind. And when he began working his first job outside of the home, he began speaking out for his co-workers. Whenever he felt something wasn't right, he always looked to remedy it. Whether that was confronting his boss whenever he felt his coworkers were not being treated fairly, or on the many occasions he felt his piecework paycheck did not amount to the efforts he had put into the job during the previous two weeks. Mark was making his thoughts known in no uncertain terms!

Al soon took notice of Mark's spirited encounters with various people, as well as through his own personal conversations with him, and began to wonder if Mark was being called to a higher purpose. Al opened up about a specific conversation in which he challenged Mark to do some soul searching of his own.

Al fondly recalled that conversation, saying, "One day riding in the car, I asked Mark: What do you think your purpose is in this life? Mark thought for a while and then asked me, Dad, what do you mean by purpose?" Al continued, "I told him that we all have goals and wants in this life, but God has things he wants us to do for Him. So, He gives each one of us a certain talent so that we can achieve His goals here on earth. And it's up to us to know the talents that God has given to us so that we may convert them into strengths in order to help Him achieve His goals here on earth." But Mark's only response was "Ok".

Smiling with both a sense of deep love and admiration for Mark, Al concluded his revelation, saying, "Several weeks went by and one day Mark said to me: Dad I know what my purpose is! However, at that point I had already forgotten our conversation, but Mark clearly had not." Mark continued, "Dad I want to be a Motivational Speaker and help my friends with disabilities have a real job and a real life just like me!" And from that day forward, Mark has been acutely aware of his very own purpose in this life.

In achieving his purpose, Mark has been led to both inform and inspire people from across the country. He loves to talk to parents and inspire them to expect great things from their child who may have a disability. Whenever he is asked by a parent for any advice on how to raise their own special child with Down syndrome, Mark will simply look deep into their eyes and say, "Just love them like you do your other kids!"

His basic message to parents is to have high expectations for their child, to treat them the same as their siblings, and to determine their God-given talents, while helping them to turn those talents into strengths. Mark firmly believes we all have value, and that we all have a purpose. And he knows God doesn't make mistakes!

Mark believes that everyone should have the opportunity to live a good life. One in which they are allowed and encouraged to reach their full potential. And where everyone can have a real job and receive a real wage.

Mark's message is not limited to only those with Down syndrome, but to everyone who has a disability. He has devoted his life to speaking out on behalf of anyone that is being hindered because of a disability, from receiving their own Respect, Opportunity, and Inclusion. This is Mark's version of what R.O.I. really stands for.

As an example, Mark has even worked with the ARC of Indiana to visit nursing homes and workshops to spread his message of encouragement and to advocate for additional opportunities for them. Mark longs for employers to understand the reliability and effectiveness of any potential employee that may have a disability. And how they can have a positive impact on their company's financial statement, in addition to the joy they naturally bring to the job.

Using his five years as a successful and beloved greeter at Walmart, Mark received the opportunity to travel through the state of Ohio talking to various Walmart store managers about the advantages of hiring individuals with disabilities.

Mark has been the face of the Work To Include initiative in Southern Indiana. His likeness has been used on billboards around the city to increase awareness of this government program that provides employers with everything they need to know in order to start an inclusion program within their business. More information on this vital initiative can be found at www.worktoinclude.org.

Many large companies, such as United Parcel Service (UPS) and Walgreens just to name a few, have already implemented their own version of inclusion programs that specifically hire and train successful employees who happen to have a disability. These companies are obviously innovators that have learned the secret to making money while tapping into an overlooked and underutilized workforce just waiting for an opportunity to prove their worth! Several of these companies are members of an organization called Disability:IN. More information can be found at www.disabilityin.org.

Mark hopes that lawmakers will continue to address the needs of those with disabilities. And he remains outspoken on the changes that still need to be made. Mark continues to speak up for those who cannot speak for themselves.

When asked what he wanted people to know about those with Down syndrome, as well as those with other forms of disabilities, Mark responded, "People need to know we can do it, we can do it!" He went on to passionately say, "We need real jobs with real pay!" And he concluded his answer by saying, "We can live on our own and make our own decisions!"

Mark not only deeply believes in these things that he professes both publicly and privately, but his life has been a shining example for all to see the truth, and the proof, behind his statements.

With all that Mark has accomplished, both personally as well as professionally, there remains one life long quest that Mark is still working on accomplishing. And that is to find the girl of his dreams and to ultimately marry her!

As mentioned before, Mark doesn't give up on a dream. And to this day, Mark still will not accept a roommate as he continues to believe that one day like his brothers, he too will be married. And why not? Have we not learned anything of the power of God and what He can accomplish when He finds someone with unshakeable faith? Like the faith that Mark and his parents have demonstrated their entire life.

Greg, reflecting back over the events shared in this book, and how he along with his brothers Mike and Todd have had a front row seat to the greatest miracle they will more than likely ever see in their lifetimes, revealed a deeply personal shift that occurred to him.

Greg explained, "Over the course of my life, I have often wondered what Mark will be like in Heaven. How God would finally take away his Down syndrome and truly make him just like his brothers. But now it has occurred to me, that Mark won't be the one changed in heaven. It will be the rest of us that will change to become more like Mark!"

Mark continues to look for speaking engagements across the country as he is driven to encourage, to motivate, and to reassure the world that those with Down syndrome really can do it! He knows that these special people can do whatever they put their mind to, when given a chance to try, the freedom to fail, and the encouragement to get up and try again.

Mark is convinced, and has personally demonstrated, that those with Down syndrome, along with others with so called disabilities, make the most loyal, able, and dedicated employees for those companies with the intelligence and foresight to recognize this largely untapped labor pool.

That is why he continues to speak up for those who cannot speak for themselves. And He continues to advocate for laws that level the playing field for those who are asking only for an opportunity to prove their worth, and to be given an opportunity to live a full and independent life!

Mark is currently working to build a following of people who are looking for ongoing encouragement by producing a series of VLOGs. These short videos feature Mark covering various topics that address the needs of the Down syndrome community. In addition, they provide personal insights into the man who truly is a living miracle. These Vlogs, video clips containing talks and interviews, podcasts, support materials, as well as links to other important organizations helping those with disabilities, can be found on Mark's website at www.markjhublarspeaks.com.

If your organization is interested in hearing Mark speak live and in person, you can also learn how to do that on his website as well.

Now you too know the story of "A Miracle Named Mark." And in true Mark Hublar fashion, he would like to conclude this book in the same way he lives his life. And that is by leaving you with some words of encouragement. Mark, along with his dad, wrote the following poem that he likes to recite as he closes out many of his presentations, entitled Imagine:

Imagine a place with no bullies, it is easy to do
Just include everyone in your kindness
And it will come back to you

Imagine everyone with a real job, it's not hard to do
People with Disabilities can be included
And can make money too

Imagine everyone with an education, it is easy to do
People with disabilities need to learn
So include us too

Imagine everyone with a social life, it can be done
People with disabilities should be included
So they can have fun

Imagine everyone living on our own, it's easy to see
If it includes you
Then it should include me

Imagine equal rights including everyone, it's easy to do
Laws can be changed
And it can begin with you

You may say that I'm a Dreamer, but it is easy to see
Being included
Is what matters to me!

Acknowledgements

I must first acknowledge Jesus Christ whose Holy Spirit was the motivating force for not only the telling of this story, but more importantly for the creation of the lives within this story. It was He who provided the thirteen chapter titles years before this book had even begun to be written, and who provided the guidance throughout the writing of this book. So, thank you Jesus!

I want to thank my parents, Buddy (Al) and Linda Hublar, for demonstrating what true love and acceptance of family actually looks like. Actions always speak louder than words, and we had a front row seat to both. Thank you for not allowing us, nor yourselves, to treat Mark any different than the rest of us. As a result, we do not see him any different then ourselves, except for maybe having a little more sense.

A special thank you goes to my wife Lisa, who is not only the love of my life, but who is also the stabilizing force that quiets my soul just with her presence. Her untold hours of simply sitting quietly with me as I typed away, stopping and asking her opinion or input on various thoughts and paragraphs, allowed me to enjoy this year long process!

A big thank you goes to everyone mentioned in the book, especially those who provided direct input. Your stories provided incredible insight and was instrumental in bringing life to these pages. This is not even mentioning the positive impact you have had directly on Mark's life!

Lastly, I want to thank the "Mark's Proof Readers" group which was comprised of both immediate and extended family members who identified and corrected the countless mistakes that could only be made in such numbers from a first-time writer. Your attention to detail was the important finishing touch that this book most definitely had to have!

"I love you All" - Greg